JAMES BALDWIN: THE DARK REALITIES OF RACIAL FERMEN

JAMES BALDWIN: THE DARK REALITIES OF RACIAL FERMEN

MUZAFAR AHMAD BHAT

SMART MOVES E 5/11, 2nd Floor, Bitten Market Bhopal-462038 M>P, India

Contents

Book Title: James Baldwin: The Dark Realities of Racial Ferment in America

Book Author: Muzafar Ahmad Bhat
Published by SMART MOVES
E 5/11, 2nd Floor, Bitten Market
Bhopal-462038
India

Printed and bound by SMART MOVES
E 5/11, 2nd Floor, Bitten Market
Bhopal-462038
India
p-ISBN: 978-81-935930-0-4
e-ISBN: : 978-81-935930-3-5
This edition published in: 2018 ISBN (ISBN Pending)

SMART MOVES

India. USA.

p-ISBN 978-81-935930-0-4

e-ISBN 978-81-935930-3-5

Preface

African-American literature from approximately 1940 to the mid-1970 was primarily a masculinist enterprise dominated by Richard Wright's protest novel and Ralph Ellison's literary pluralism. It can be surmised that along with Alice Walker, re-discovery of Zora Neale Hurston and the pastoral tradition, the last two decades have witnessed an explosion of writing by black women and the recuperation of a black female literary history that dramatizes a specifically urban sensibility suggested by the novels of, among others, Nela Larsen, Ann Petry, and, of course. Toni Morrison. In the process, Baldwin's novels have been relegated to the archives of the unread, cast aside in favour of the lapidary, famously polemical essays. The novels, however, despite their poor critical reception, are interesting because they rarely capitulate to the urge for a simplified rhetoric that characterizes the essays of the early 1970s, persistently retaining the unresolved tension and complexity of a writer- a gay black writer no less-divided between his role as a popular spokesman for the race and his role as an artist whose imaginative life encompasses aesthetic standards that may alienate a popular audience. The novel form partially liberated Baldwin from the pressures that, he felt as an essayist answerable to frequently hostile audience, both black and white. Baldwin's work, moreover, suggests a cultural space where the trend in black literary history to polarize itself along gender lines might be reversed.

James Baldwin displays the nature of his own specifically artistic quest, which includes the search for the real, and the development of his personality as an artist. He impresses the readers by his powerful, moving and ennobling account of the nature and development of his extra-ordinary soul. He describes his struggle against the perverted human contexts in which he grew up. His experiences vividly explain what sources of strengths were needed to protect his own individuality, innate talents, and his humanity from dissipation and degeneration. His dilemma was essentially that which has always faced that artist who is also, consciously or not, committed to a specific social problem. Baldwin endeavours through his art to express the enduring truth of human experience. The quest for the real takes its birth in a drive which pushes one into the depth of ordinary, everyday occurrences and opens out to the extra-ordinary dimensions of life, it unveils the real, which is to be found in and through the essential core of one's experience.

Baldwin aimed at demonstrating a certain competence in dealing artistically with the raw material of his experiences: his commitment was to see his aesthetic and social responsibilities as constituting a whole that does not discard the meaning of his experience and his desire to express this in an artistically satisfying way. To him the development of a purposeful public voice was as essential as the formulation of an artistic vision of life. With his experiences Baldwin accomplished the artistic freedom while creating order out of disorder to create an artistic platform for himself.

As an artist Baldwin followed his own bruised past and tradition and actualised upon him the art of using one's past artistically. The inability to face one's history means a lack of maturity and Baldwin is of the view that the black is ill-treated in America because history is written in the colour of his skin. This is the central fact in the history of America. No matter how much he must suffer in America, no matter how much he fears and hates the torture rouse into which he is cast, Baldwin realizes that, he must live in America. It is only after his return from Europe then he makes his odyssey to the south that he is able to appreciate the positive results, the strength and beauty of the people who have suffered slavery and the most appalling social and economic inequalities.

Whether one believes every sordid detail of Baldwin's particular experiences or not, his portrait of black life in general impresses the readers as true. Baldwin does not exaggerate the dread, despair and depravity of the lives of the blacks in America. Through his artistic portrayal Baldwin makes the readers wonder what sort of commitment and strength could have overcome the forces seeking to knock him down. Protest literature, Baldwin argues, is false because it seeks to deny man's freedom; and its murky sentimentality, and the tendency to offer the facile explanation of man as a social being devoid of all complexity are the defects of such literature. Protest fiction and the naturalistic novel treat man as a simple product of biological and environmental determinism. They deny the possibility of escape from these external forces. Fantasy and escapism are unknown elements in the actual lives of black people, but the literature that presents and interprets their life is firmly rooted in realism. The black writer seeks to present a picture of experience and also attempts to re-order the chaos of reality.

All art may be seen as protest by virtue of its commitment on the one hand to offer mechanical reproduction of reality and on the other to suggest a radical revision of that reality. Baldwin's views on the hidden truth of the protest novel are well-known. Far from being to tool for liberation, the protest novel merely perpetuates the false image of blackness, an image that the white American cherishes. Baldwin explains the psychological necessity for the white man to construct an image of black inferiority and to hold this image between himself and the truth. Paradoxically the image reflects not black reality but white guilt.

Prof. Dr. S. Karthik Kumar

Assistant Professor

Annamalai University

Acknowledgements

Indeed it is first my venture to publish a book which was really a dream we fantasized long ago and it would have really ended up a dream had I not been encouraged and guided by my guide Dr. S Karthik Kumar Assistant Professor Dept of English, Annamalai University.

I deem it my humble duty to register my sincere gratitude to Prof. Dr. S.Manian, Vice-Chancellor, Annamalai University, for showering his benevolence and best wishes upon me.

I would like to place on record my deepest gratitude to Dr. K. Arumugam Registrar, Annamalai University. I owe him a debt of gratitude for his wishes and guidance.

I express my warm thanks to Dr. E. Selvarajan, Dean, Faculty of Fine Arts, Annamalai University, for his advice in bringing out this book.

It is my heartfelt wish to place on record my deepest sense of gratitude to Dr. K. Muthuraman, Professor of English, Dean, and Faculty of arts Annamalai University, for being well wisher.

It is my privilege to thank Dr. K. Rajaraman, Professor and Head Department of English for his valuable suggestions that helped me a lot in shaping the book.

My special thanks to Dr. A Selveraj, Dr, D. Shanumugam, Dr. J Arul Anand, DR. C. Santhosh Kumar, Dr. M.V, Siva Kumar Associate Professors of English Annamalai University for his benevolence and love.

My thanks goes to Dr. V K Saravanan, Dr.M.Madhavan, Dr. K. Ganeshram, Dr, P. Dinakaran, Dr. M. Soundharajan, Dr. G. Aruputhavel Raja,Dr. R. Palanivel, Dr. R. Suresh Kumar, Dr. B.

Karthikeyan, Dr. T. Deivasigamani, Dr. C. Shanmugasundaram, Dr, K. Padmanaban Dr. P. Premchandar Dr.S Ayyapparaja, Dr.V.Gnanaprakasam, Dr, D. Shanumugham, Dr,.C Santhosh Kumar, Dr. S Sundarajan, Dr. N. Saravanaprabahar.

My heartfelt thanks go to Dr. R. Vijaya, Dr.A. Glory. Dr. S.P. Shanthi.Dr.Aruna Devi. Dr. S. Bhuvaneshwari and Dr. S. Florence., Dr. K.N Sharmila, Dr. R Sankari, Dr. R .Bharathi.

I would like to thank several people who helped me in the course of writing this book. They include colleagues, friends and family, students and scholars, my editor and editorial assistants.

I would also like to thank my dear friendS Mr Imtiyaz Ahmad Mir, Tanveer Hussain Bhat, Mohd Asif Bhat, Zahid Manzoor, Sajad Ahmad Ganie, Irshad Ahmad Dar, Dr. Rayees Ahmad Rather, Dr. N Shaik Hameed, Danish Ahmad Mir, I would like to thank my parents without whom i was not possible to accomplish the making of this book.

My special thank goes to Mushqoor Ahmad Bhat and Zulfkar Ahmad Bhat who are always there to support me . I would also place on record my special thanks to Deviya Zaffu who helped me in every possible ways in publishing this book.

1

Introduction

It is not our differences that divide us. It is our inability to recognize, accept, and celebrate those differences. – Audre Lorde

The hegemonic white culture and discourse in America had ruled the African Americans out of the ambits of political representation and publication while perpetuating deep-rooted false notions about them. Consequently, the construction of racial identity or the communal development of African Americans have been tested by their struggle to unleash themselves from the debilitating social and psychological effects of the dominant racist ideology and culture and this revolutionary change can be noticed very much from 18th century poet Phillip Wheatley to Toni Morrison, Maya Angelou, Walter Mosley, Alice Walker, Gloria Naylor, and Paule Marshall, the contemporary top Black writers. Afro-American early writers also helped the Afro-American Black writing move forward. Fredrick Douglass, American reformer, social orator, writer and statesman, is one of them. He escaped from slavery, and became the leader of the abolitionist movement, gaining note for his dazzling oratory and incisive antislavery writing. The issue of slavery and the subjects related to slaves such as adaptation to the new situation, slaves' objections, and breaking free from captivity have been a dominant theme at the time of slavery. Most of the writings at the time of slavery were autobiographical. Consequently, these autobiographical works written by slaves were named slave narratives. The slave narratives were the outcome of the conflicts between the southern Whites who supported slavery and the northern slaves who were seeking freedom from the oppression of slavery in the middle of the nineteenth century. A review of Afro-American literature from slave narratives to the writings of the present modern Black writers will help us to examine the logical links and connections in Afro-American literature.

James Baldwin was born on August 2, 1924, and educated in New York. Baldwin's father was a pastor who subjected his children to poverty, abuse, and religious fanaticism. As a result, many of Baldwin's recurring themes, such as alienation and rejection, are attributable to his upbringing. Living the life of a starving artist, Baldwin went through numerous jobs, including dishwasher, office boy, factory worker, and waiter. In 1948, he moved to France, where much work originated. Baldwin published *Go Tell It on the Mountain* in 1953. A largely autobiographical work, it tells of the religious awakening of a fourteen-year-old. Besides this, his childhood experiences, his experiences as a black man and a homosexual highly inspired such works such as *Giovanni's Room, Nobody Knows My Name*, and *Another Country*.

Baldwin holds a respectable place in American history as one of the foremost writers of both black and gay literature. He was an active participant in the Civil Rights movement. His first novel, *Go Tell It on the Mountain*, appeared in 1953 to excellent reviews and immediately was recognized as establishing a profound and permanent new voice in American letters. "Mountain is the book I had to write if I was ever going to write anything else," he remarked (Interview to Paris Review 1984). Baldwin's play *The Amen Corner* was first performed at Howard University in 1955 (it was staged commercially in the 1960s), and his acclaimed collection of essays *Notes of a Native Son,* was published the same year. A second collection of essays, *Nobody Knows My Name,* was published in 1961 between his novels *Giovanni's Room* (1956) and *Another Country* (1961). The appearance of *The Fire Next Time* in 1963, just as the civil rights movement was exploding across the American South, galvanized the nation and continues to reverberate as perhaps the most prophetic and defining statement ever written of the continuing costs of Americans' refusal to face their own history. In 1964 *Blues for Mister Charlie,* his play based on the murder of a young black man in Mississippi, was produced by the Actors Studio in New York. That same year, Baldwin was made a member of the National Institute of Arts and Letters and collaborated with the photographer Richard Avedon on *Nothing Personal,* a series of portraits of America intended as a eulogy for the slain Medger Evers. A collection of short stories, *Going to Meet the Man,* was published in 1965, and in 1968, *Tell Me How Long the Train's Been Gone,* his last novel of the1960s appeared. In the 1970s he wrote two more collections of essays and cultural criticism: *No Name in the Street* (1972) and *The Devil Finds Work* (1976). He produced two novels: the bestselling *If Beale Street Could Talk* (1974) and *Just above My Head* (1979) and also children's book *Little Man, Little Man: A Story of Childhood* (1976). He collaborated with Margaret Mead on *A Rap on Race* (1971) and with the poet-activist Nikki Giovanni on *A Dialogue* (1973). He also adapted Alex Haley's *The Autobiography of Malcolm X* into *One Day When I Was Lost.* In the remaining years of his life, Baldwin produced a volume of poetry, *Jimmy's Blues* (1983), and a final collection of essays, *The Price of the Ticket.* Baldwin's last work, *The Evidence of Things Not Seen* (1985), was prompted by a series of child murders in Atlanta. Baldwin was made a Commander of the French Legion of Honour in June 1986. Among the other awards he received are a Eugene F. Saxon Memorial Trust Award, a Rosenwald fellowship, a Guggenheim fellowship, a Partisan Review fellowship, and a Ford Foundation grant. James Baldwin died at his home in Saint-Paul-de-Vence in France on December 1, 1987.

African American Literature is a literature produced in the United States by Americans of African descent. The literature attained its height with slave narratives and the Harlem Renaissance. The Great migration of African Americans during the world wars produced a new sense of independence in the black community and the black writers, and impelled to make an effort to end segregation and racial discrimination in their fictional and non-fictional works by bringing the recurring themes such as combating racism, searching for a black identity, and maintain a unique quality of life in public. In the arena of this literary world, James Baldwin occupies a daunting place to be reckoned with major great writers of the world.

Baldwin's work from the late 1940s to the 1980's sought to exploit a masculine repertoire of morality and ethics to depict the nature of human agony. Baldwin's literary works grapple with the social and aesthetic challenges of being Black in a world that has systematically denied and devalued one's existence. It is over and against this problematic existence in which James Baldwin's works raises tragic questions of identity and ethical paradox in the present age.

This book grapples with a black aesthetics and the pangs of affliction affiliated to black aesthetics, and at the same time offer a potential roadmap for engaging in and theorizing about black existence at the intersections of race, gender, class from the vantage point of literature (the novel). In other words, this thesis rejects allegiance to any one thinker or body of thought because, as Communication Studies scholar Sha-nara Reid et al (2013) argues, "black experience is multiple, contingent and contextual, single methods or theories of resistance could not possibly offer an effective response to anti-blackness". (*Shanara* Reid-Brinkley lecturing WGA DF) By examining the suffering and by extension the trauma that are experienced in James Baldwin's major chunk of novels under discussion deliberates upon the question raised by DuBois nearly a century ago; "What means black suffering"? (2). It can be argued that the blues expression of psychological and emotional pain in these narratives not only to draw attention to the suffering individual, but more importantly, accents the various ways that Black people have responded to systematic and normalized dehumanization. Through the encounters with their wounding, some characters are completely destroyed and alienated by their suffering while others transform their pain into something positive. On the other hand, it can be gleaned from Baldwin's text a philosophy that black suffering is multiple and can be debilitating but can only be transcended when those experiences are shared with others who are suffering under and near the margins of that society. Thus, the task at hand in Baldwin's works is more than an assertion and exposition of suffering and trauma, but a dialectical confrontation with what it means to be a human being whose fundamental humanity is called into question by a racist and sexist society.

This book addresses the dearth of scholarship on the particularities of black suffering which holds no allegiance to any theory or theological sensibilities. Instead, it foregrounds the black interior, scholars can move from the everydayness of pain and suffering to a more nuanced and useful methodology for discussing the literary and lived psychology of black Americans. My investigation draws from various disciplinary perspectives so as to free inquiry from disciplinary decadence and moves into an approach that can entertain all the questions brought to the fore by the presence of black suffering. How Baldwin confronts an existential reality that is steeped in both the faith and humanistic tradition. Thus, any useful discussion must take into account the question of domination and liberation at the same time. Furthermore, a great deal of scholarship on Baldwin tends to view the writer with a resultant backdrop of connective narrative that documents those painful aspects of being black in a white world.

Moreover the second chapter elaborates upon the various narrative technicalities. As language has the ability to accommodate conceptions of truth and cognition and the extendibility of language, the way and it can be steadily elaborated and unfolded. Most important rich analysis of what Baldwin calls the problematically abstract and the problematically concrete. However by the side of the problematically abstract, language sometimes seems full of the weight of the world. By the side of the problematically concrete, language can seem inappropriately quick and cavalier. Belligerent postmodern attempts such as verbal irony and jazz are being taken throughout the works as part of the belated nature of trauma and manifested in the narrative structures of all the texts, to destabilizes and blurs distinctions between past and present, which, in turn, leads to time as a continuum with no distinct beginning, middle, or end.

Throughout this book a deep reading is carried out regarding the black existentialist leitmotifs in which attempt is being made to foreground black existence as being not only problematic, but a form of resistance in and of itself. Such a read will take into account the intellectual and cultural tradition that has grapple with domination, suffering, and trauma that is grounded in the blues tradition. An effort is made to carve out a framework that situates the black experience within a blues context-a context that encompasses multiple and competing responses to white domination.

Furthermore, Frantz Fanon's *Black Skin, White Masks* is feasible to be taken into account as Fanon explores the condition of being black in a white world. Armed with tools of psychoanalysis and modern European philosophy, his work is more than an intellectual exercise. Fanon wants to create a world where black and white can live together in a state of psychological health. Like Sartre and Camus, he is committed to using his mind to further a better world. Thus, in the tradition of African Critical Theory, philosophies, theories, and perspectives that have assisted black folk in our quest for human freedom and liberation, Baldwin makes every conscious and unconscious effort to comply and follow it in black and white.

A decent starting point in the analysis of black aesthetics seems to be the feeling of identity crisis, of depersonalization following social alienation of the individual. There is, in the contemporary period, an acute spiritual tension whose roots go back, on the one hand, in the profound economic and political changes of the twentieth century and, on the other hand, in the accumulation of cultural information that subliminally presses on the psychic of the modern writer. Regardless of the reasons behind this identity crisis, the modern self seems bound to reinvent itself, to adapt to the requirements of a new social reality. An important part of this thesis focuses around to the concept of dignity and social acceptance, the evolution of the intellectual being analyzed here in close connection with the evolution of morality, religion, and the triumphal march of the principles of equality and liberty. Openness or cultural relativism is the new social policy of the United States. It is obvious that every political regime tries to educate its citizens in the light of its guiding principles (in the case of democracy, the principle of equality and acceptance of the other, each with his own standards and own perspective) and the public enemy of the contemporary society becomes the discriminator, who cannot accept diversity and the multitude of points of view. However, when there is no more shared vision on the public good and there are no more common goals, the question rises whether the social contract is still possible. What this dissertation tried to prove is that contemporary society has dissolved into a mass of separate individuals, each pursuing his own selfish goals and subjective interests, destroying that common vision and that social and moral order necessary for the construction of a healthy image of the self. Because the formation of the individual or, in a narrower sense, of the modern intellectual, cannot be understood other than in close relation with society, the redefinition of the modern self becomes synonymous with the redefinition of the moral standards of society, seen, most of the times, as an impossible mission, hence the nihilism or pessimism of many analysts .What is relevant for this chapter is the fact that the writer under scrutiny here do not perceive this transition as a moral or philosophical failure, but as a fresh start, where the modern self is not only freed from the old limitations, but assumes new identities, better adapted to the challenges of the white color dominated society. As indicated in the theoretical chapters consciously James Baldwin being aware that America needs a profound transformation and that the key to this transformation is a correct balancing of individual rights and obligations. The true identity cannot be forged other than in relation with the others, assertive or conflictual, but necessarily infused with respect for the other, thus ensuring the climate of social dignity required for a correct functioning of society.

The proper starting point for any critical discussion about suffering must take into account the psychological, physical, social, and economic terms under which Black Americans have been decentred. The thesis examines the literary work of Baldwin's work that chronicles the painful and catastrophic narratives of black people, the depths of woundedness and suffering from the outset of the text. Such a display forces a probing of the moral and ethical consequences of white anti-black racism as well as Black anti-black hatred. More critically, the novels highlights the effects of both external and internalized rejection of excessive blackness and the highhandedness to which it contributes to an inability to negotiate one's existential reality.

"For to survive in the mouth of this dragon we call America, We have had to learn this first and most vital lesson-that we, were never meant to survive. Not as human beings".--Audre Lorde (Sister Outsider 56)

African American literature has become an inevitable part of American literature and culture. The strong presence of African American literature has paved the way for the emergence of Native American, Asian American, and Chicano American streams of literatures. It is only with the significant representation of African American literature American society stands to be cleansed from the problem of racial discrimination. African American literature has examined the problem of racial discrimination in all its philosophical, existential and epistemological aspects. It has travelled from mid eighteenth century with slave narratives to the current times with all its socio literary exuberance initiating a literary and cultural transformation in the fabric of American society.

It was only during the mid twentieth century after the ground breaking influential socio political texts Washington's *Up From Slavery* (1901) and Du Bois's *The Souls of Black Folk* (1903) and Zora Neale Hurston's *Their Eyes Were Watching God*, Richard Wright, Ralph Ellison and James Baldwin devised a brand of African American Modernism. Right's *Native Son* (1940), Ellison's *Invisible Man* (1952) and Baldwin eloquent volume of essays *The Fire Next Time* argued for social and cultural emancipation of African Americans. Cutting above the influence of Civil Rights Movement that were taking place simultaneously, it is only James Baldwin who addressed the issues of Black masculinity, sexuality and the gay rights of African Americans. Exploring the psycho sexual problems, Baldwin has deconstructed the sexual myths that legitimized the discrimination and served as a projection of insecurity and fear of white people. He has rejected Black Nationalism and diverted the attention of the society towards dissolving the contradictions that plagued African American society. This perspective has paved the way for a more analytical and critical elucidation of African American society in the late twentieth century. The emergence of African American Women writings brought in double jeopardy of racism in Black Women's movement. Gloria Hull examined the dilemma of Black women in *All the Men are Black. All the Women are White, But Some of Us are Brave.* This has made many black women to turn toward each other for a better introspective and analytical understanding of Black Women's problems. Maya Angelou's *I Know Why the Caged Bird Sings* (1970) and Tony Morrison's *The Bluest Eye* (1970) addressed the question of how self-identity and respect is achieved by a black girl in a society, which hardly values her existence. Tony Morrison expanded her thematic range from female identity to Black people relationship with African American past in her works *Song of Solomon* (1977), *Beloved* (1987) and *Jazz* (1991). These novels have explored folk heritage, slavery and mother hood. This is followed by Alice Walker's *The Third Life of Grange Copeland* that discussed the issues of poverty and family violence. She exposed the contradictions within the Black movement depicting the issue of domestic violence, father daughter rape and female genital mutilation in *The Colour Purple* (1982) and possessing the *Secret of Joy* (1982). Despite the negative representation of Black men, Alice Walker's works have initiated the renaissance of African Women's writings. This has paved the way for the emergence of literature of place, small towns, and neighbourhoods and of home. Many creative writers who are veterans of black movements and black feminism assisted by activist stance provided insightful literary and political essays. Gloria Naylor's *The Women of Brewster Place*

(1982), Audre Lorde's *Zami* (1982), Paul Marshall's *Praise Song of the Widow* (1983) and Gayle Jones *Corregidora* (1975) have redrawn the map of African American literary canon. The younger writers like Sherley Ann Williams with a sensitive portrayal of African Women's life in *Dessa Rose* (1986), Terry McMillan with *Waiting to Exhale* (1992) broke the new ground in the genre of fiction for Black women. Amidst the great wealth of Black women's creative production, African American Men's writing has been receiving less attention. Yet the autobiographical resonances and the sharing of the themes continue to hold the significance and relevance African American Men's writings. John Edgar Wideman's *The Homewood Triology, Philiadelphia fire* (1990), *Brothers and Keepers* (1984), Charles Johnson's *The Middle Passage* (1990), *The Oxherding Tale* (1974) have charted out African American counter history. All these works have proved that African American literature has unleashed a new creative talent on par with other significant streams of Post Colonial and Post Modern literatures.

Elucidating African American literature has become a challenging task to every critic and academician. There is a good deal of African American literary theory even before the advent of Post-Colonial, Post-Modern streams of literary criticism. The usual criticism levelled against African American literary criticism is that it tends to be programmatic and prescriptive. All the significant African American writers chose to employ an appropriate mode of representation to advance the cause of African American creative expression. Du Bois, Alain Locke, Richard Wright tried to propose a theory of reading rather than a particular format of criticism. This perspective has undergone a rapid transformation, with the advent of European schools of thought in the American Academy. Beborah E. McDowell in the essay *"The Changing same"* describes the arrival of the theory as a changing paradigm shift in African American literary study. Many of the African American critics have expressed their displeasure at the grand imperative of modern theory such as semiotics, structuralism, post structuralism, psychoanalysis. Crawling underneath the rubble of critical theory, African American critics have set to rebuild the format of creative expression. Expressing a mixture of hostility and enthusiasm some of the Black scholars have managed to establish remarkable understanding of new theory, which led for radical change. Instead of considering theory as a threat to their activism, they perceived it as a potential for social change and great philosophical foundation.

However this perspective was welcomed by a whole new generation of African American students, who graduated from prestigious white universities with a conceptual clarity on modern literary theory. The new breed of academic critics encountering difficult conditions, tried to recover the broken past by drawing sources from Marxism, Feminism, Post Structuralism and Psychoanalysis. Eventually African American literary criticism has become a discourse to be reckoned with.

The first theoretical essay in African American literary study is Barbara Smith's 'Toward a Black Feminist Criticism' (1982). It has opened a new line of thinking on Feminism and Black Feminism. Smith has postulated the interweaving of gender, class and racial politics essential for Black Feminist perspective. She argued that Black Feminist critics should have a good knowledge of the identifiable tradition of Black Women's writing. She should have a good eye and ear for Black Women's language and she should think and write out of her own identity. Black Women critic is not supposed to graft the ideas or methodology of white literary canon. Smith has demonstrated these principles in response to counter the homophobia in literary representation.

The Post-structuralism has exerted considerable influence on Black Feminist Criticism and it has also changed the perspectives of African American male critics. Houston Bake and Henry Louis Gates Jr., giving up their former anti theoretical stance, have become potential African American Post-Structuralists critics. The Journal started by these people

'*Black American Literature Forum*' (1967), has become the focus of the theory of debate and became a podium to discuss many of the contradictions. Houston Bake conceded the critical weakness of Black Arts movement and the need of a new theoretical paradigm. He strongly opposed the imposition of new theoretical paradigm and sought for the liberation of African American cultural theories imprisoned in the hands of prominent white scholars. He expressed his allegiance to the holistic, cultural –anthropological approach implicit in Black Aesthetics. Baker's conversion to Post-structuralism was obvious in his *Blues, Ideology, and Afro-American Literature* (1984). This book was subtitled as *Vernacular Theory* signalling his commitment to vernacular Black tradition and to a systematic mode of thinking. Baker took the Blues as his matrix for a vernacular theory, arguing that the Blues are the multiplex, enabling script in which Afro American cultural discourse is inscribed. The pervasive use of Blues matrix is seen in his *Modernism and the Harlem Renaissance* (1987) which argued for complete revision of modernism in the light of African American art forms and the literature of Harlem Renaissance.

Henry Louis Gates for some time had been engaged in translating Post-Structuralists insights for African American Critical use. In his books *Figures in Black. Words, Signs, and the "Racial" Self* proposes the vernacular practice of 'Signifying'. Bringing in various means of 'signifying', he makes it as a kind of verbal trickery. It is conveyed as an indirect means of expression and power relations. It is this self conscious, self-knowing; self-reflexive African American literary tradition Louis Gates has generated achieved a distinctive critical following. However, Joyce Ann Joyce in *New Literary History* (1987) contests his theory. In her article The Black Canon: Reconstructing Black American Literary Criticism, she attacked Gates finding his writing sterile and elitist. According to her Gates ignores the fact that African American history had a vital role in resistance and emancipation. However, there is confusion in accepting the theory as it is understood to be a homogenous entity against the plurality. Barbara Christian examines the negative obverse of theory in her essay "Diminishing Returns: Can Black Feminism(s) Survive the Academy?" (1994.)

Afro-centrism begins with the premises that African American people are primarily of African descent, despite their century's long existence in the United States. Afrocentrists believe that all the people of Black diaspora share a common heritage and they are conceived in terms of African culture. Molefi Kete Ashante in *Afrocentricity* (1988) has promoted the theory of Afrocentricity. It is in the light of these perspectives; the works of James Baldwin need to be elucidated. The critical and theoretical issues that are part of the evolution of African American literature and criticism are aptly reflected in the works of Baldwin. He has transcended the common themes of African American literature and portrayed the issues of multiculturalism that continue to influence the life of African American in the contemporary situation. His attempt to initiate the relevance of theoretical application to the gay and lesbian issues of African American lives is almost obvious in all his works. His theoretical stance, apart from the proposed theories of Louis Gates, Baker and Barbara Smith, brought in the militant representation of African American social and cultural issues. Through his works, he emphasized on the process of activity rather than fixed outcome. Though, autobiographical mode is well rooted in African American thought, he has not depended much on autobiographical mode except on the remnants of autobiography. Other writers like Frederick Douglass, Alice Walker theorized the material and psychic conditions of slavery in their autobiographical narratives. Since 1980's Afro American, critics have used theory in variety of ways. One of the significant critics Hazel Carby in *Reconstructing Womanhood: The Emergence of Afro American Woman Novel-*

ist (1987) established a unified notion of feminist tradition and criticism. Carby's approach invoked British cultural studies and is associated with the emergence of Stuart Hall, Kobena Mercer and Paul Gilroy. In contrast to African American centrism, theoretical projects have projected crises crossings of ethnicity, nationality, class and gender. Gilroy's *The Black Atlantic* (1993), Kobena Mercer's *Welcome to the Jungle* (1994), Judith Butler's *Gender Trouble* reconceptualised the repeat performances of African American biological and cultural identities.

The literary and critical survey of African American literature offers the cross racial, cross-cultural scholarship necessarily for literary excellence and human importance. The possibility of distinction between white culture and black is discovered in a satirical and theoretical enterprise that does not objectify African American writing. James Baldwin can be located in the midst of the plethora of emerging theoretical streams and the contradictory contentions that try to establish African American literature as the 'discourse of the other'. Generally, Black literature is synonymous with literature of protest. They protest against exploitation, limitations, restrictions, discrimination, intolerance, inequality etc to which they are subjected by the Whites in the United States. As is amply clear by now, Black literature springs from the life of the Black people and it records the experiences of Black life. In fact, life of those who come from Black race is as human as it is of any other race and is in no way inferior to the life of other races. According to DuBois:

> Negro art is today ploughing a difficult row. We want everything that is said about us to tell of the best and highest and noblest in us. We insist that our Art and Propaganda be one. We fear that evil in us will be called racial, while in others it is viewed as individual. We fear that our shortcomings are not merely human. (The Crisis 55)

Black Art is representative of the Black condition and shows their experience in America. It demonstrates the reality of the Black life in American society. As Ron Karenga said:

> Black art, like everything else in the black community, must respond positively to the reality of revolution. It must become and remain part of the revolutionary machinery that moves us to change quickly and creatively.... Black art must expose the enemy, praise the people, and support the revolution. . . . It must be functional like the poem of another revolutionary poet ... it must be collective. In a word, it must be from the people and must be returned to the people in a form more beautiful and colorful than it was in real life. (Du bois and the color line: Race and class in the age of globalization" 141)

Undoubtly black writing speaks about sociological, ideological, political and cultural situations created by an unjust oppression, repression, harshness and marginalization of the Blacks in the States. The earliest duty of the Black writers is to recover and improve sublimit by invoking and reorganizing a heroic African past. Black writer doesn't pay any attention to the reflexes of the behaviour of others, especially of the White community. They had started writing about Blacks with pride and pleasure. Langston Hughes (1926) in his essay "The Negro Artist and the Racial Mountain" pointed out:

> We younger Negro artists who create now intend to express our individual dark-skinned selves without fear or shame. If white people are pleased we are glad. If they are not, it doesn't matter. We know we are beautiful. And ugly too. The tom-tom cries and the tom-tom laughs. If coloured people are pleased we are glad. If they are not, their displeasure doesn't matter either. We build our temples for tomorrow, strong displeasure doesn't matter either. We build our temples for tomorrow, strong as we

know how, and we stand on top of the mountain, free within ourselves. ("The Negro Artist and the Racial Mountain" 9)

There are two kinds of Black writers in America: 1) those who were expatriated to Europe like Richard Wright, James Baldwin, Chester Himes, William Gardner Smith and 2) those who remained in America like Amiri Baraka (LeRoi Jones), Toni Morison, Alice Walker, Zora Neale Hurston etc. Black fiction in America contained a world of mass culture and yet it has neither been a product of mass culture nor did it contain those elements which put such a culture at odds with art. Black writer's effort is to record the struggle of the Blacks during their long journey. Negroes played an important role in American life, art, literature, culture and history and their relationship to America dates back to days even before 1619 which means it is as old as America itself. Black literature in America is the literature of reality and of facts and everything written in the name of Black literature refers to the Black community in the States. Also Black literature is literature of protest against white racism in American society.

Abraham Lincoln and Martin Luther King, Jr. the two famous Americans who fought against racism, discrimination and they too had to suffer quite a lot for Black emancipation. Abraham Lincoln, as the President of America, signed the Emancipation Proclamation for Black American people on the 22nd day of September, 1862 A. D and making it a point that slaves be emancipated in best possible ways. However, slavery was not abolished immediately and in some states like Texas, Blacks remained in bondage until 1865. Emancipation neither brought real freedom nor relief to them from the stigma of colour.

African American literature and art have had an economic origin, i.e., this literature originated as a result of the slave trade which was basically an economic activity. One of the earliest slave narrative writers was Gustavus Vassa from the present-day Nigeria. He wrote a slave narrative entitled The Interesting Narrative of the Life of Olaudah Equiano or

Gustavus Vassa. Those African slaves who had escaped from slavery in the South came in the North and started to write about their miserable life. If we go deeper into the history of African American life, it can be seen that it is full of discrimination, inequity, suppression, segregation etc. Vassa was born in 1745 and was brought into America when he was just eleven years old. Later, he left America and went to England. Black writers created protest literature and challenged the system of slavery.

After the post-slavery era or the end of American Civil War, some of the African American writers continued to write about the condition of the Black people in the United States. Even after Abraham Lincoln's announcement in 1862 of emancipation of slaves and even after the actual statutory passing in 1863 of the Emancipation Proclamation, many Blacks had difficulties in finding jobs and supporting themselves. While in the South, living conditions for the Blacks were far more terrible than they were in the North. The Blacks were still discriminated against by most of the White people and they were restricted and segregated time and again during this period. Because of these conditions, more than one million Black Southerners migrated to the Northern part of America because the situation in the Northern America was slightly better for the Blacks since in the North they could find better jobs, send their children to better schools and could even vote. But there were so many problems like racism that remained unsolved.

W. E. B. DuBois was one of the outstanding writers among them and was also one of the most influential Black American Civil Rights activists, leaders, critics, authors, orators, and scholars of the first half of the nineteenth century. He was also one of the Black activists who joined the Communist Party and was also the first African American to earn a Ph. D. from Harvard in 1895. He had an important influence on the Civil Rights Movement of the 50s and the 60s. He published a 24 collection of his essays in which he described as to in which conditions Black people lived in the country. In a book authored by Howard Zinn and Anthony

Arnove, DuBois is quoted to have said: "The problem of the twentieth century is the problem of the color-line" (The Souls of Black Folk 114)

Harlem Renaissance, which is said to have existed from 1920 to 1940, represented the flourishing period of African American literature, music, dance, visual arts and culture in general. The area namely Harlem in New York City was the centre of Black social and cultural movements in the United States and it is well-known for the production of Black literature. The most famous writers in the period of Harlem Renaissance included the poets like Countee Cullen, Arna Bontemps, Langston Hughes and Claude McKay, novelists like Rudolph Fisher, Zora Neale Hurston, Nathan Eugene (Jean) Toomer, James Weldon Johnson and Jessie Redmon Fauset. At this time many of the Black writers and artists, especially who lived in Harlem, started producing a great variety of fine and original works dealing with African American life and culture. Black readers were greatly attracted to and influenced by these works.

Harlem Renaissance became known as the era of 'The New Negro Movement 'or 'The New Negro Renaissance'. *The New Negro* was the title of an anthology edited and published in 1925 by sociologist and critic Alain Locke. The term Harlem Renaissance was borrowed from this anthology. The Harlem Renaissance exalted the unique culture of African Americans and redefined their expression. It was a period of remarkable vigour and creativity at the centre of New York's Black ghetto. According to Steven Watson:

> African-American writing existed before these years, of course, and many authors who first found their voices during the 1920s produced significant work in the years following. But the New Negro's organized, self-conscious phase lasted less than a decade.(16)

The writers of the Harlem Renaissance describe the reality of Black life in America and their struggle for racial identity. They explained the life of African Americans in the rural South and the urban North. Harlem was the centre of urban Black life. It was considered as the heart of African American life. It was as a symbol of an African American's desired living conditions during the early twentieth century. Moreover, the Harlem Renaissance movement of the antic nineteen twenties was really inspired and kept alive by the interest and presence of white bohemians. It faded out when they became tired of the new directions of the movement

Harlem community was the centre and spiritual godfather and midwife of the Harlem Renaissance. During the period of the Harlem Renaissance, there have been a number of remarkable Black writers who wrote about cultural emancipation of African Americans and fought strongly against slavery and the unjust American society. Resultantly, Harlem almost became a holy place for the Blacks and a centre of the Black community in America. The best protest stories by Negro writers were written at this time. They challenged all the cultural values, beliefs, concepts of beauty, ugliness and White-made social problems of the Black people. Steven Watson reveals that:

> The New Negro movement embraced more than literature: it included race-building and image-building, jazz poetics, progressive or socialist politics, racial integration, the musical and sexual freedom of Harlem nightlife, and the pursuit of hedonism. (28)

In this era, a great number of novels, short stories, plays, poems, and articles about the Blacks by Black writers were published. Southern Black musicians brought jazz with them to the North and to Harlem. The Harlem Renaissance was a significant period even for Black music because of great musicals written by remarkable Blacks like Duke Ellington, Louis Armstrong, Bessie Smith, Dizzy Gillespie, and Charlie Parker and, hence, Harlem Renaissance also came to be called as the Jazz Age.

The Harlem Black communities included American Blacks and many West Indian Blacks. More than ten thousand Blacks in Harlem protested against violence, Black misery, American unjust society, discrimination, towards the Blacks by the Whites and so on. In 1920, Harlem had obtained a symbolic significance for Blacks and it was the centre of Black protest and Black political activity. Steven Watson further points out:

> "Simultaneous with the establishment of Harlem as the Black mecca, political organizations proposed their strategies for race-building. Chief among them were Marcus Garvey's African nationalist movement, the Universal Negro Improvement Association, the National Association for the Advancement of Colored People, and the socialist African Blood Brotherhood".(43)

During this era, many Black Americans come to stay in Harlem although they had basically migrated from the rural, agricultural South to the urban industrial centres of the North like Harlem. Majority of the Blacks who came to North of America settled in Harlem. Among them there were musicians, writers, artists and so on. Therefore, Harlem became some kind of a hub of literary, cultural sophistication and artistic talent.

W. E. B. DuBois edited the magazine entitled "The Crisis" which was published by National Association for the Advancement of Colored People (NAACP). One more important monthly magazine of the period entitled Opportunity was edited by sociologist Charles S. Johnson and was published by the National Urban League (NUL). These periodicals were quite instrumental in creating awareness among the Blacks in this era. About DuBois, Steven Watson stated, "A social scientist and political leader, Du Bois was also Harlem's first culture czar" (The Crisis 12)

About the positive changes that the Renaissance brought about in the lives of the Blacks, Alain Locke stated:

> The younger generation comes, bringing its gifts. They are the first fruits of the Negro Renaissance. Youth speaks, and the voice of the New Negro is heard. ...Here we have Negro youth,

with arresting visions and vibrating prophecies; forecasting in the mirror of art what we must see and recognize in the streets of reality tomorrow, foretelling in new notes and accents the maturing speech of full racial utterance. (10)

Most of the commentators claim that 'The New Negro Movement' was successful in creating foundational steps in the age-old African American arts tradition. But some others believe that the Renaissance was a failure. The major themes of the Black Arts Movement included love, beauty, ugliness, identity, Blackness, humiliation, historical phases, changes, music, cultural phenomena etc. A theme that seems to be running throughout almost the whole of African American cultural artistic productions is the theme of the preservation of Black culture, Black identity and it further includes dealing with guilt, social effects of race, shame, gender, class distinctions, violence, coming to terms with White standards of beauty etc. Black art related itself to historical, economic, educational issues as well as to social growth and development of a people.

However, during the Second World War period, Black writers in America, like other writers in the country, started to write about the war. But in the post-war period, Black writers started writing about new aspects of African American life; they wrote about the living conditions of Black people in America. Civil Rights Movement refers to the equal treatment to be given to all citizens of America irrespective of their race, gender, class, colour etc and it also refers to laws which invoke claims of positive liberty. The African Americans also resisted and protested against racial segregation and discrimination by adapting to strategies such as civil disobedience, non-cooperation, non-violent resistance, protests etc. In the era of Civil Rights Movement, Black activists struggled for getting freedom, ending segregation, racism and projecting a new understanding of Black Nationalism. The Civil Rights and Black

Power movements created a powerful impression on Black voices in the 60s.

The late 1940s of African American writing was a period dominated by a writer like Richard Wright. He was powerful with words and the images which he created about the Blacks and Black life in America and he had also immensely influenced other Black writers of this period. The Age of Richard Wright began after the Harlem Renaissance, i. e. around the 1930s and continued to the end of the 1950s. Further, the 1960s was a period in which James Baldwin dominated African American writing. He came out as a major voice of the African Americans in the times of Black Power Movement which grew out of Civil Rights Movement. Baldwin re-established the personal essay to its place as a form of creative literature. He was a well-known Black writer whose work addressed race and sexuality. As the Civil Rights Movement progressed, it was supported and fortified across the country by groups such as Black workers, communist organizations, Black membership in unions, Black artists, creative writers and socialist groups like the League of Revolutionary Black Workers and the Black Panthers.

On leaving the US for Europe, James Baldwin may have sought after racial invisibility, but he ended up becoming the most visible African-American writer of his time. Half in earnest, one can subscribe to the claim that Baldwin has become what he travelled four thousand miles not to be: a 'Negro writer. The young James Baldwin expatriated to Paris to prevent himself, in his own words, "from becoming merely a Negro; or, even, merely a Negro writer". (Native Son 13) In Paris he tried to resolve what appeared to be the necessary choice between individuality and collective enrolment by finding formal and substantial ways not to choose. One way, another scholar maintains, was to become an intellectual, that is, to craft an essayistic voice that seemed unraced, a voice that sound sensibility with a purpose.

The cosmopolitan image of James Baldwin seems supported by that fact that his literary hero, Henry James, cultivated an analogous national ambiguity as a sign of being a highly civilized, trans-national individual. However, Baldwin is no cosmopolitan, quite the contrary. In a Freudian sense, cosmopolitanism is the repressed element of essentialism; although erroneously associated with a position of color-blind universalism, cosmopolitanism is best described in terms of color-curious rather than color-blind or color-bound. In what color references are concerned, James Baldwin rather belongs to the color-bound category. In taking after Henry James, Baldwin is forcing a divorce from his other literary hero and main source of oedipal anxieties, Richard Wright. Ironically, cosmopolitanism is a position more accessible to Richard Wright than to the color-bound James Baldwin, and the prevalence of the Negro problem in Baldwin's writing of America in Europe testifies to that. Baldwin's mastery of the form of essayistic writing, which reminds one commentator of ideal French literature, cannot be used to obscure the content of his writing; at most it can serve to illustrate the writer's multiple cultural self-framing and, eventually, to highlight the schizoid experience of an African American intellectual whose racial allegiance may come at odds with his personal dream of individuality.

Notwithstanding to all this tension between the affirmation of individuality and the need for communal enrolment forms the subject of Baldwin's first and most acclaimed volume, *Notes of a Native Son* (1955), a collection of ten essays plus an introduction, divided into three parts. The first part of *Notes of a Native Son* contains literary and film pseudo-criticism – not because of its lack of formal and substantial quality, but because the subjects of Everybody's Protest Novel, *Many Thousands Gone(Ira Berlin. 1998)* and Carmen Jones: *The Dark is Light Enough(1955)*, are mere pretexts bringing forth an argument on the "Negro problem." Whereas the first part takes literary discourse as its reference and establishes Baldwin's argumentative persona, the second part takes social discourse as its reference and offers three more razorblade-like essays unweaving the oppressive social fabric: The Harlem Ghetto, Journey to Atlanta, and the central *Notes of a Native Son*. The essays in the third part, namely Encounter on the Seine: 'Black Meets Brown, *A Question of Identity*, 'Equal in Paris, and 'Stranger in the Village, take his European travel as a reference; Baldwin's stay in Europe forms the source and material of the four texts and is important not so much in itself, as (re)placement, but because it permits the displacement and contemplation of the self by placing Baldwin's discussion of (black) America on a European background.

In his writings, James Baldwin displays the nature of his own specifically artistic quest, which includes the search for the real, and the development of his personality as an artist. He impresses the readers by his powerful, moving and ennobling account of the nature and development of his extraordinary soul. He describes his struggle against the perverted human contexts in which he grew up. His experiences vividly explain what sources of strengths were needed to protect his own individuality, innate talents, and his humanity from dissipation and degeneration. His dilemma was essentially that which has always faced that artist who is also, consciously or not, committed to a specific social problem. Baldwin endeavours through his art to express the enduring truth of human experience. The quest for the real takes its birth in a drive which pushes one into the depth of ordinary, everyday occurrences and opens out to the extra-ordinary dimensions of life, it unveils the real, which is to be found in and through the essential core of one's experience.

Baldwin is of the view that the black is ill-treated in America because history is written in the colour of his skin. This is the central fact in the history of America. No matter how much he must suffer in America, no matter how much he fears and hates the torture rouse into which he is cast, Baldwin realizes that, he must live in America. It is only after his return from Europe then he makes his odyssey to the south that he is able to appreciate the positive results, the strength and beauty of the people who have suffered slavery and the most appalling social and economic inequalities.

Whether one believes every sordid detail of Baldwin's particular experiences or not, his portrait of black life in general impresses the readers as true. Baldwin does not exaggerate the dread, despair and depravity of the lives of the blacks in America. Through his artistic portrayal Baldwin makes the readers wonder what sort of commitment and strength could have overcome the forces seeking to knock him down.

Baldwin in his fiction presents his characters with their faults and strength, as full human beings, not as propagandistic caricatures of good and evil. He has recognized the danger to artistic and realistic rendering of character that is presented with an intention of propaganda. He was committed to present his characters without minimizing their faults or extrapolating their virtues. His writings may serve as a powerful weapon in a just cause, but the fact that it is essentially a protest does not deter him from telling the story of his own soul. His writings besides telling the story of the development of his personality as an artist, reveals what his life may have in common with the lives of others. It show how Baldwin is moulded, through a struggle with stifling and hostile forces and gives the meaning of his artistic endeavours and achievements.

The unique feature of his style is his tendency to relate his personal life and experiences with whatever commentary he offers on social and moral questions. His caustic comments on social realities evolve directly from his personal experiences. He, therefore, speaks with an authority. His astonishing flow of high eloquence is denounced by critics as speech-maker's prose. Baldwin seems to have lost respect for the novel as a form, and his great facility with language serves only to ease his violations of literary strictness. Like Baldwin's stepfather, Johnny, the protagonist of

Go Tell It on the Mountain was an incongruous mixture of piety and cruelty. "Everyone had always said that John would be a preacher when he grew up, just like his father" (16). But Johnny, like Baldwin, "would not be like his father, or his father's fathers. He would have another life." (18) Baldwin committed himself to be a writer. This eventually made him famous.

The relationship between fiction and truth is that of antagonism since the two are not in complementary disposition. And so if veracity can be associated with fiction, it has to be on the basis of "Aristotelian probability and necessity". But beyond the fecundity of the writer's imagination; beyond the fertility of his inventiveness, the writer sometimes unconsciously transcends fictionality to some candour. And this said truism (high artistic truth) presents in the work a pseudo-social discourse with a functional message for the psychological, historical and instinctive dimensions of our empirical existence in this world of reality.

Seeing that art interprets all human experiences, the novelist debatably assumes the role of an artist, a teacher, a philosopher, a psychologist, and a concerned cognoscente who propagates and reproduces the values of his time. This is the role that James Baldwin played for Africans with his writings. Thus, the novel presents to us a social discourse that creates awareness on our human condition. This condition is that the fevered effort by Africans to exorcise the racist tendency of the imperialists is also inherent in the Africans themselves. This cultural role of the novels now projects a palpable alternative thought pattern that reflectively re-engages the novel in a different light, quite contrary to the existing musings and analytic models in which such novels have been analyzed.

However as a matter of fact, beyond the social discourse dimension, the truth of Baldwin's fiction is in the psychological conflict of the characters that reveals internal contradictions and quest (heterodoxy) that characterize the supposed coherent self. Baldwin's novels fictionalize fundamental personal questions and dilemmas amid complex social and psychological pressures thwarting the equitable integration of not only blacks, but also of gay and bisexual men, while depicting some internalized obstacles to such individuals' quests for acceptance.

This book evaluates the racial ferment in America and how James Baldwin's novels, namely *Go Tell It on the Mountain* (1953), Giovanni's Room (1956), *Another Country* (1962), *Tell Me How Long the Train's Been Gone* (1968) and *If Beale Street Could Talk* (1974) try to grapple with it and how James makes use of the motif of racial ferment and limbo of sexuality to dramatize 'complexes of the years of denigration and self-abasement'. While confronting the sexual polarization of American society in *Go Tell It on the Mountain*, Trope of homosexuality and heterosexuality both in *Giovanni's Room* and *Another Country*, the dynamics of moving out of ethnic group to practice alternate sexualities to overcome the race divide is minutely brought out in both *Tell Me How Long the Train's Been Gone* and *If Beele Street Could Talk*, conterminously making his voice fully realised according to Ian Watt, Chinua Achabaean 'preeminent sociality' and 'exceptional historic representativeness' profuse in James Baldwin's novels.

Go Tell It on the Mountain (1953). Set in Harlem in the late 1930s, the novel describes a day in the life of 14-year-old John Grimes, the son of Gabriel, a fierce Pentecostal preacher, as he struggles with his growing sexual awareness and the warnings of the church that thunder through the novel: "You is in the Word or you ain't - ain't no half way with God."(13)

But while aggressively critical in places of Pentecostalism's rigid distinctions between the saved and sinners, the spirit and the flesh, Baldwin's novel is tinged too with nostalgia and wonder. The description of John's conversion as he wrestles on the threshing floor is a testimony to the church's ability to destroy and renew: "John did not feel the wound,

but only the agony... only the fear; and lay here, now, helpless, screaming, at the very bottom of darkness."(56) As Baldwin said in an interview with the *Village Voice* in 1985, "terror of the flesh... is a doctrine
which has led to untold horrors". Throughout *Go Tell It on the Mountain,* he emphasises the physicality of worship and the thin line between
religious and sexual exertion. As the storefront congregation worships,
"their bodies gave off an acrid, steamy smell" (67) which is not far off
the "the unconquerable odour ... of dust, and sweat surrounding the "sinners" (72) in the street outside. During worship, as Baldwin repeatedly
reminds us, the physical body can be hidden but not forgotten behind the
holy robes: Elisha's "thighs moved terribly against the cloth of his suit".
(77)

While writing his second novel James Baldwin had recently immi-
grated to Europe undoubtly felt that the effects of racism in the United
States would never allow him to be seen simply as a writer, and in fact,
he would have feared that being tagged as gay would mean he couldn't
be a writer at all. In *Giovanni's Room,* David is faced with the same type of
decision; on the surface he faces a choice between his American fiancee
(and value set) and his European boyfriend, but ultimately, like Baldwin,
he must grapple with the alienated culture that produced him. In keeping with the theme of social alienation, this novel also explores the topics
of origin and identity. As the title of the novel suggests, Giovanni's room
(his bedsit in Paris) is a powerful symbol in the text and one that acts as
a representation of David's emotional state. In the early stages of the relationship, David acknowledges the limitations of the space but accepts
it. However as David feels his masculinity being smothered by Giovanni,
the room becomes an oppressive symbol; something he must escape if he
is to regain his misguided masculine identity. The symbol of the room
is particularly interesting considering the novel's subject matter. In the
novel, David is engaging in his first public homosexual relationship and

it could be seen as his first forays into officially "coming out". However it is curious that Baldwin frames this by juxtaposing David's new found sexual freedom with the physical restrictions of Giovanni's room. This idea is encapsulated in a quote from the novel: "But it was not the room's disorder which was frightening; it was the fact that when one began searching for a key to this disorder one realised...it was a matter of punishment and grief" (66).

As such, *Giovanni's Room* poses questions of nationalism, nostalgia, and the constitution of racial and sexual subjects in terms that are especially resonant for contemporary identity politics. Set in 1960s New York City bohemia, *Another Country* cuts into the white liberal psyche and reveals the destruction that benevolent racist actions cause to blacks. It also tells stories of how blacks cope with internalized racism, the desire to love whites, and the violence they find themselves committing against them. *Another Country* is an amazing title. It is a metaphor for the territory of other people that characters struggle to love. Traditional heterosexual, interracial, and homosexual relationships alike are strained as they struggle with prejudices from within and unforgiveness all around them. Characters are drawn to each other, but aren't always aware of the oppressive forces that shape their attraction. Baldwin's characters struggle with the discovery or suppression of the true meaning of their love for one another "People don't have any mercy. They tear you limb from limb, in the name of love. Then, when you're dead, when they've killed you by what they made you go through, they say you didn't have any character. They weep big, bitter tears - not for you, for themselves because they've lost their toy". (123)

However Vivaldo, the white protagonist, reflects on his relationship with Rufus: "He had refused to see it, for he had insisted that he and Rufus were equals. They were friends, far beyond the reach of anything as banal and corny as color. They had slept together, got drunk together, balled chicks together, cursed each other out, and loaned each other money. And yet how much, as it turned out, had each kept hidden in his heart from the other!...Perhaps they had been afraid that if they looked too closely into one another each would have found....the abyss. Somewhere in his heart the black boy hated the white boy because he was white. Somewhere in his heart Vivaldo had feared and hated Rufus because he was black" (134).

Baldwin's insistence on a sexualised spirituality remains radical today. As he wrote in *If Beale Street Could Talk* (1974), "when two people... really love each other, everything that happens between them has something of a sacramental air"(55). In Baldwin's view, it is the loving (and often sexual) touch of another person, not God, who "saves" another human being. Baldwin wrote in *Tell Me How Long the Train's Been Gone* (1968), "then one respects the pain of others, and so, briefly, but transcendentally, we can release each other from pain." (44) The novel consists of three books without chapter divisions: *The House Nigger Is there anybody there? and Black Christopher.* Baldwin in various interviews makes it clear that his own life was the basis of much of Tell Me as it was for his first novel, *Go Tell on mountain.* About the autobiographical element in his novels, it can be estimated that, Baldwin writes out of one thing only that is his own experience, the trials and tribulations he has gone through in a white dominated society which for that matter was hardly willing to accept the aura surrounding the black aesthetics who by dent of their sheer hard work made world to listen to them.

It is a common claim that a culture of one's own is a condition for the achievement of identity; but what culture means in the first place and in what sense it could be one's own are questions worth posing. One African-American writer who never tires to ask such questions is James Baldwin. This thesis offers a close reading of the title personalisation and quest of identity While Baldwin, the writer spent most of his life in quest of a harmonious ontology, his texts from a symbolic and avant-gardist point of view reflects the quest for an ontological harmony in artistic senses. This paper argues that there is a definite triadic ontology in the construction of his self through his characters. This expresses itself in a number of ways ranging from the setting, thematic concerns, character development to structural and stylistic construction. The gist of my argument is that conflicts and tensions develop between oppositions, in quest of a kind of synthesis and harmony. Thematically, this expresses itself in such oppositions as sensuality and abrasive racial ferment, primitivism and modernism, sensation and perception etc Baldwin reaches unexpected conclusions on self and community.

However in order to bring his individual and collective identities to a common purpose, Baldwin aims at locating himself, as clarified in *Notes of a Native Son,* "within a specific inheritance and to use that inheritance, precisely, to claim the birth right from which that inheritance had so brutally and specifically excluded me" (12). In his time, he culturally consecrated the competing racial claims of (black) inheritance and (American) birth right, the former limited and limiting, the latter vast and boundless, as the access gate to the "kingdom of culture," in W.E.B. Du Bois' words. However, a number of figures in the post-Harlem Renaissance made their way to the kingdom of culture through other gates than James Baldwin, by constructing a significantly different relation to their roots. Charles Johnson, for instance, affirmed polemically that "all knowledge, all disclosure, all revelation from the past, from our predecessors, black, white, and otherwise, is our inheritance… Any sense that other human beings have made out of the world… all that is what we have inherited as human beings" (Passing the Three Gates: Interviews with Charles Johnson 66) Hence there is no striving to enter the kingdom of culture, for one is already in residence. Nevertheless, while in historical hindsight Baldwin's troubled black dialectic of birth right and inheritance may prove less relevant, it continues to provide an idiosyncratic insight into what could be the mirror stage in the formation of African American identity: the recognition of the other. Even progressive intellectuals of the Harlem Renaissance never really understood the importance of black history and culture to the United States and did not regard the relationship between whites and blacks as central to the story of the republic, the white immigrant and frontier experiences were central to an Americanism unaware of the centrality of the self-other confrontation in its emergence. It took James Baldwin to highlight, in prophetic rhetoric, the role of the white-black dialectic in the making of an American identity. Consequently, James Baldwin has often been said, in accusatory tone, to speak mostly to a white readership, and that is true in the sense that the message he conveys is shaped for both white and black ears: Baldwin's colored rhetoric aims at demonstrating that the identity crisis of the Negro is a crisis of the whole America. In Baldwin's essays, the question of color identity comes to pose the deepest epistemic and ontological questions not only to the African American, nor only to the black writer who flees to Paris, but also to his apparently sheltered white readers, pushed out of what Butterfield calls their "tragic innocence." Americans who are ignorant of black identity are ignorant of their own, concludes Butterfield, much like Baldwin himself (Black Autobiography in America 187)

2

Transcending the Nondescript Definitions of Self Image

The era of stubborn intolerance towards homosexuality, *Giovanni's Room* is considered a controversial novel since it openly depicts same-sex love and desire that could not be accepted easily at that time. Far from the issue of racial identity that is the focus of Baldwin's other works, *Giovanni's Room* exposes the complexities of sexual, national and gender identity and the psychological and emotional troubles that one may face when the authentic self does not fit the dominant ideal of national identity. Thus, the novel marks Baldwin's transition from racial issues that are mainly addressed to a specific community he belongs to, to wider issues of human identity regardless of race differences. Baldwin would later assert that "American writers do not have a fixed society to describe. The only society they know is one in which nothing is fixed and in which the individual must fight for his identity." (A Biography 11) This chapter will follow the protagonist's struggle with his sexuality in *Giovanni's Room*. It will show that in his quest for the self in which he rejects aspects of his identity, the main character, David will ironically lose his true self. His attempts to match pre-established codes that will guarantee his status of being a white American male contribute to deepening his alienation. Leading the life of an expatriate in France, just as Baldwin did at the time of the novel's publication, David is exiled from his homeland as well as from his inner self.

Giovanni's Room, as the title suggests, has metaphorical significance for the story David is telling. It is cluttered with the debris of Giovanni's life—an unhappy past in Italy, an uncertain future in France, a superficial present of drinking and pandering among a subculture characterized by gossip, jealousy, and scandal. Just as Giovanni satisfies David's repressed desires, so does he find in David meaning and hope, and his room becomes, alternately, a haven or a prison, an Eden or a hell, a passing way to truth or a dead end, for both young men. *Giovanni's Room* is an intimate, confessional narrative of an American named David who looks back on his turbulent experiences in France on the eve of his return to the United States. The novel works through two time frames simultaneously, for as past events are recounted, the relevance of the present moment gradually emerges. By the end, night has become morning, and only then does the story being told reach its conclusion.

Months earlier, David came to France with his girlfriend Hella, but uncertainty in their relationship and her wanderlust sent her traveling solo to Spain. David, with little money and none forthcoming from his father in the United States, befriends and exploits the generosity of a middle-aged homosexual, a Belgian American businessman named Jacques. With him he moves through the world of Paris gay bars, and at one of them he meets a handsome Italian bartender named Giovanni.

David and Giovanni have an immediate rapport, and on the night of their meeting they stay out until dawn under the patronage of Jacques and Giovanni's boss Guillaume; they end up alone back at Giovanni's room, where they embark on a sexual relationship.

Having little money, David moves in with his new lover. Though David has had homosexual feelings and experiences before, the intensity of his fascination for Giovanni, and his own position in life—nearing thirty, and, ostensibly, marriage with Hella, makes his relationship with Giovanni new and threatening. As so often has happened in the past, David ignores the possible consequences of his actions and continually reminds himself of his freedom, at any point, to abandon this new situation. Throughout the telling of this history, the narrative returns to David's present in a rented house in southern France, alone, without either of his lovers. Time passes slowly; he measures the hours of the night drinking, preparing to leave, thinking mournfully of Giovanni, and waiting for morning to come. He recounts his panic and denial at Giovanni's growing dependence on him. Upon receiving news of Hella's imminent return from Spain, he cavalierly seduces a woman acquaintance, for whom he feels no desire, to prove his independence and control. When Hella arrives, David abandons Giovanni; though they run into each other, he never admits to anything more than a casual friendship. Hella is puzzled but attributes David's behaviour to the ambiguities of life in exile.

Giovanni's Room chronicles its protagonist's search for his sexual identity. The search proves to be futile, and the novel ends on a note of considerable hopelessness. David, now living in France, is revealed first through a flashback, in which the reader learns that he grew up in Brooklyn with his father and his father's sister, Ellen. David's mother died when he was five years old, but her presence has been a real one. Her picture dominates the living room, and David frequently has dreams about her that are both Oedipal and necrophilic. He does not reveal the real nature of these dreams to anyone. When he wakes up screaming, he merely tells his father and aunt that he has dreamed about a graveyard. The flashback also recounts David's relationship to Joey, his closest school chum. One night, when David is staying at Joey's house, the two boys fall into each other's arms and have a sexual experience that is highly satisfying to both of them. In the morning, however, David leaves and, because of his guilt, refuses to see Joey for the rest of the summer. When they finally meet at school in the fall, David treats Joey cruelly. Their friendship is destroyed.

After high school, David works, but he soon tires of the life he is living, and he sails to France, largely trying to run away from himself. The bulk of the novel is devoted to telling of his life in France, where, in a gay bar in Paris, he meets Giovanni, an Italian who works there. When the bar closes, David and Giovanni accompany Jacques and Guillaume, two aging homosexuals, to Les Halles for a breakfast of oysters and wine. Then David goes with Giovanni to Giovanni's room. Once they are there, Giovanni pulls David down to him on the bed, and the sexual relationship that is to continue for some months begins. David's thoughts about it are, "With everything in me screaming No! Yet the sum of me sighed yes."(87) The first two parts of the novel shows David's uncomfortable acceptance of Giovanni's love. Soon, however, the squalid room becomes for David a symbol of what he sees as the squalidness of his relationship with Giovanni, the squalidness of homosexuality. David begins to feel trapped in Giovanni's room.

At a crucial point in the novel, Hella, with whom David had an affair in Paris and to whom he has proposed marriage, writes from Spain telling David that she will marry him. David immediately has a sordid affair with Sue, an overweight American girl, to prove to himself that he is still capable of having sex with a woman. Eventually, in desperation, Giovanni submits to Guillaume's sexual overtures in order to get back his job at the bar. This submission, however, leads to tragedy: An enraged Giovanni strangles Guillaume and, after a week of hiding out, is apprehended. He is given a swift trial, found guilty, and sentenced to death. While all of this is happening, David takes Hella to the south of France, again trying to escape from his homosexuality. He tries to lose himself by having sex with her constantly, but soon he grows tired of her and is repelled by her body. Hella discovers David in a gay bar with a sailor, which makes her realize what the nature of his relationship with Giovanni had been. She leaves David and sails for the United States. On the morning of Giovanni's execution, David is in the house where he had lived with Hella in the south of France. This scene provides the frame from which all the novel's several flashbacks in the novel occur. David locks the house, starts away from it, tearing up the envelope in which the news of Giovanni's impending execution has reached him. He throws the scraps into the breeze, but the wind blows some of them back onto him.

Giovanni's Room begins with David standing in a great house in the south of France, looking at his reflection in the window as night falls. As he stands, drinking what will be the first of many drinks before the night ends, he casts his mind back over the chain of events leading him to the most terrible moments in life, and however his former lover Giovanni will die on the guillotine. The novel, divided into two parts, is one long retrospective view of David's life, a series of brooding flashbacks that rehearse the story of his failed attempt to resolve his sexual identity crisis and understand his betrayal of Giovanni. With his former fiancée headed back home and his former lover sentenced to death, David is left alone to sort out his past life in order to see what he can make of his future. His nightlong vigil leaves him facing the dawn with a "dreadful weight of hope."(224)

While he regards his face in the darkening glass, he conjures up images of his early years in America, particularly his first homosexual experience with a young friend, Joey. He has always refused to admit the significance of this potent and defining event, lying to himself and everyone else to evade the shame of the "beast" inside that threatens to condemn him to an "unnatural" life. He fears the force of his awakened sexuality and adopts a pattern of flight to avoid coming to terms with it—flight from an interfering aunt and a distant, adulterous father, from meaningless friendships and pointless jobs. He finally flees his country, with the half-formed thought that in Europe, in Paris, he will discover and understand this identity that has so far only frightened and confused him. In Paris, David falls in with the vaguely bohemian crowd of young expatriates, flirting occasionally with the gay world he knows through an older homosexual acquaintance, Jacques, but remaining proudly above what he sees as its dirt and shame, yet he is lonely and unsatisfied. Prompted by persistent concerns about his manhood, David rather flippantly asks an American art student, Hella, to marry him. While she is in Spain considering this proposal, however, David meets Giovanni in a seedy gay bar; it is this handsome young Italian bartender who forces David to confront his sexual fears and ambivalent desires. Terrified but ecstatic, David spends the night in Giovanni's room. He capitulates at last to the "morning stars" of Giovanni's eyes: "With everything in me screaming No! Yet the sum of me sighed yes."(87) So part 1 ends with David's reluctant but growing acceptance of his homosexuality and Giovanni's love. In part 2, David turns from that acceptance, and in doing so denies himself and a world of bright possibilities with Giovanni.

The blissful months David and Giovanni have, living together in Giovanni's crowded little room, are not enough to free David from his confusion. When Hella returns, the room begins to seem claustrophobic and dirty, another thing to flee. He does flee, taking up with Hella again and leaving Giovanni jobless and in great emotional pain. Giovanni's love is passionate, violent, and complete. It both exhilarates and terrifies David because it demands an equal intensity in return. This David cannot give. When they stand, each with a brick in his hand, they could kill each other or embrace each other. It is a decisive moment. David is paralyzed. His only response is flight, and he runs away with Hella. His escape, however, comes at extreme cost: In despair, Giovanni murders Guillaume, his predatory former employer, and is sentenced to death. It is only on this last night of Giovanni's life that David can confess that he loved Giovanni; but extracted so late, this confession can provide only a filament of hope for David's future.

In *Giovanni's Room*, Baldwin colourfully depicts the life of certain Paris milieus, but his focus is primarily on the three characters in the lovers' triangle. The dialogue is peppered with phrases of French that add atmosphere and reinforce the sense of anonymity and ambiguity so crucial to David's sensibility. Baldwin explores his chosen themes—bisexuality, exile, self-deceit, and guilt—with candour and boldness, remarkably so, given the age in which he wrote. The tone of the novel is one of rigorous self-examination and honest resignation; David has come to accept, although too late, responsibility for his actions. As such, his growth through the novel is a passage into maturity, a painful and tragic loss of innocence. Baldwin's biographer, Fern Eckman, quotes the author as saying, "David's dilemma is the dilemma of many men of his generation, by which I do not so much mean sexual ambivalence as a crucial lack of sexual authority."(99). Therefore, concerns about sexual authority, as seen in nearly all the characters in the novel, are a controlling theme in *Giovanni's Room.* Social determinism directs the course of the characters' lives, and Giovanni comes to his unfortunate end largely because of the economic determinism that forces him to submit sexually to Guillaume, by whom he is so repelled that he loses control and strangles him.

The yoking of the secular and the sacred is what Raymond-Jean Frontain tries to do when analyzing Baldwin's novel *Giovanni's Room* (1956). In James Baldwin's Giovanni's Room and the Biblical Myth of David Frontain discusses homosexuality, traditionally seen as belonging to the secular realm, and relates it to the sacred myth of the friendship between David and Jonathan found in I and II Samuel. According to Frontain, Baldwin uses the biblical myth not only to talk about the fulfillment of love after death, something past critics have done, but also to present the possibility of men sharing greater affection for each other than they share with women. Frontain describes Baldwin's purpose in using the myth as an attempt to show that the myth was quite archetypal in nature to justify the nature of relationship between bisexuals Frontain points out what he sees as several similarities between the myth and the novel. First, the main characters are named David and Giovanni, Giovanni being Italian for Jonathan. Second, as in the biblical story, the character David grieves deeply over the loss of his friend. Third, just as the biblical myth presents Jonathan as the one showing greater love for the fictional David than David for him, so too does Baldwin's Giovanni, or Jonathan, express greater love for David than David does for him.

The interweaving of the themes of sex and death is an interesting one in the novel and a common one in modern literature. For David, every sexual encounter results in a loss. His guilt makes him shun Joey, thereby losing a valued friendship. His inability to accept his own sexuality results in his losing Giovanni and is indirectly responsible for Giovanni's death. Finally, in his inability to sustain a heterosexual relationship with Hella results in her leaving him.

He warns revolutionaries against growing bitter as they cry out for change, and he warns the faith minded against losing sight of social concerns as they seek affirmation from God. In *Giovanni's Room* (1956), Baldwin's character David places people in various groups depending on their responses to oppression: some become bitterly mad; others, insanely mad, and still others, heroic. These groups provide a means for understanding Baldwin's warnings to the marginalized. The label 'bitterly mad' might best describe revolutionaries whose response to oppression has gone awry, and the label 'insanely mad' might describe the faith minded whose response has likewise gone wrong. Baldwin suggests that both groups are forced to live with the menacing presence of oppression because in modern society, paradise, an ideal world of human equality is unsustainable. As this is the matter of fact that evident in the fact that, people are not terribly anxious to be equal but they love the idea of being superior and try to dominate other in every possible way particularly in America and such circumstances make it easy, on the one hand, for revolutionaries to become so focused on the oppressor that they grow bitter and suspicious and, on the other, for the faith-minded to so fixate on paradise—heavenly paradise—that they ignore oppression, insanely pretending that it either does not matter or does not exist. Baldwin suggests in *Giovanni's Room* that one group is just as bad as the other because their responses to oppression grow out of despair, despair over the world's inability to sustain perfection, to treat all people with fairness and dignity: Perhaps everyone has a garden of Eden, I don't know; but they have scarcely seen their garden before they see the flaming sword [that drives them out and prevents their return]. Then, perhaps, life only offers the choice of remembering the garden or forgetting it. Either, or: it takes strength to remember, it takes another kind of strength to forget, it takes a hero to do both. People who remember court madness through pain, the pain of the perpetually recurring death of their innocence; people who forget court another kind of madness, the madness of the denial of pain and the hatred of innocence; and the world is mostly divided between madmen who remember and madmen who forget. Heroes are rare.

The death of David's mother when he is five years old represents a significant loss in David's life. His recurrent nightmare about his mother is a thinly veiled and, for David, a horrible sexual enactment. Because of it, David always views sex as something putrid, unclean, and ultimately repulsive. The novel is filled with symbolism based on dirt and clutter. Giovanni's room represents to David disordered life. In contrasting David and Giovanni, Baldwin is making a generalized comment on American sexual restraint and its resultant problems as opposed to the greater sexual acceptance that Baldwin senses in other cultures. Giovanni, the Italian, even though he was once married, can live without guilt in his homosexual relationship with David. David cannot accept Giovanni on similar terms.

Through the use of flashbacks and first person narrative, Baldwin takes the reader on a journey of self-discovery in which we are introduced to the complexities of the protagonist's inner self. This journey is David's attempt to "find myself" (31) as he puts it, an expression related to the American eagerness for self invention and which suggests that "something has been misplaced" (32). This may also recall Baldwin's own situation of being black and gay in a white American society which makes him a "misplaced" individual and a stranger in his own country. James Baldwin's *Call to Service: Christian Spirituality in African-American Literature.* When James Baldwin dramatizes that a suffering individual's willingness to serve others gives him or her the power to counteract the dehumanizing effects of oppression, he reveals how Christianity can be used to understand the nature of spirituality, not only in his literary works, but also in the works of other African-American writers, particularly those who have followed him in the literary canon. This may seem ironic considering that since the nineteenth century; African-American writers have gradually moved away from Christianity, criticizing the way in which it has been a force in either condoning or ignoring oppression. Some critics have credited Baldwin with freeing later African-American writers from any concern with Christianity, a freeing that seemed to occur also in the larger African-American community outside the literary establishment. The seeming abandonment of Judeo-Christianity by the black literary establishment and by some in the larger African-American community has resulted in discussions of spirituality that frame it solely within the supernatural or within religious worship. However, in calling for societies oppressed to serve, to care for the needs of others who are oppressed and needy, Baldwin actually follows Judeo-Christianity in defining spirituality more holistically, reflecting how the black masses have historically understood and practiced spirituality and how they currently do so. And, in prizing service apart from the Christian faith wherein he learned about service, Baldwin still points the way to understanding how Christian spirituality manifests itself in the works of contemporary African-American writers.

This valuing of raising children as being male or female and establishing a safe gender identity for them is reinforced by theories viewing social influences as necessary in forming one's gender identity. Until the mid 1970s and according to available data, the individual's sense of being male or female, known as his core gender identity, was held to be mainly influenced by postnatal psychological and social interactions rather than by prenatal hormonal ones. Studies carried out at John Hopkins University by Dr. John Money and collaborators held that gender identity is mainly influenced by the sex a child is reared as. Studies were based on hermaphrodites and people with chromosomal anomalies. In such cases, what the individual learns during childhood determines his core gender identity. Many investigations sought to show the association between gender identity disturbances in childhood and the development of homosexuality during adulthood. According to Richard C. Friedman, this correlation seems to be the only way by which homosexuality could be viewed as psychopathological. (Psychoanalytic Bias Against Homosexuality: Reflections on the 1970s 5) Yet, queer theorists who came later have given altogether different perspective to come about. (— (1988)

Generally, even critics and psychoanalysts who claim to have tolerant views about homosexuality remain anxious about its development among children and adolescents. Institutions and psychologists try to cure them rather than helping them to accept and adapt to their sexual orientation. Freud was among the few psychologists who did not view homosexuality as a disease. Therefore, formulated that sexual orientation is not to be worried about as it does not affect one's mental health or ability to be a talented or successful person since world has witnessed lot of imminent people who were sexual in orientation. One may be unhappy, neurotic, torn by conflicts, inhibited in his social life, analysis may bring him harmony, peace of mind, full efficiency, whether he remains homosexual or gets changed.' Psychologists particularly Freud, believed that homosexuality is an inborn drive that is difficult to change, and he saw no need to change it since it is not a sickness. But he acknowledges the importance of helping homosexuals to be more comfortable in their condition and be socially integrated. He also rejects the view that psychoanalysis should be influenced by social standards of morality. As a matter of fact Homosexuality is assuredly no advantage, but it is nothing to be ashamed of, no vice, no degradation; it cannot be classified as an illness; we consider it to be a variation of the sexual function, produced by a certain arrest of sexual development.

Unlike the dominant views of his time, Freud's account is more tolerant and universalizing, refusing all types of discrimination on the basis of one's sexuality. In the late nineteenth century, leaders of the homosexual emancipation movement in Germany advocated the theory of the "Third Sex" (1860) that was defended by the German homosexual lawyer Karl Heinrich Ulrich, in his attempts to win equal rights for homosexuals. According to this theory, homosexuality is an inborn, biological drive. Therefore, it is unjust to condemn homosexuals for a condition that is neither chosen nor acquired, but is natural. Yet, this theory presupposes that a female soul inhabits a male body, and this is what directs towards people of the same sex. This implies that homosexuals are biologically distinct and viewed as an exception to the rule of nature according to which people are born either male or female with inborn gender identities that restrict their sexuality. Although Ulrichs' purpose in defending this claim was mainly in favour of the homosexuals' emancipation, he maintains the axiom that sexual desire must be directed towards a different sex and that those with same sex desires are having gender troubles. Homosexuality was explained by the individual's psyche and feelings that were thought to be different from his biological sex. This view was criticized by many thinkers such as James Mills Peirce who states in a letter from:

> There is an error in the view that feminine love is that which is directed to a man, and masculine love that which is directed to a woman. That doctrine involves a begging of the whole question. The two directions are equally natural to unperfected man, and the abnormal form of love is that which has lost the power of excitability in either the one or the other of these directions. It is unisexual love (a love for one sexuality) which is a perversion. The normal men love both... (The Cult of Quaternions 24

Peirce rejects the dominant view that sexual love is naturally focused on the opposite biological sex and asserts that homosexual passion is a natural and pure love just like the heterosexual love is. He adds:

> I clearly believe . . . that we ought to think and speak of homosexual love, not as "inverted" or "abnormal," as a sort of colour-blindness of the genital sense, as a lamentable mark of inferior development, or as an unhappy fault, a "masculine body with a feminine soul," but as being in itself a natural, pure and sound passion, as worthy of the reverence of all fine natures as

the honourable devotion of husband and wife, or the ardour of
bride and groom. (Science and Homosexualities 32)

This view paves the way for Freud's theory of the original libido that
gradually develops and becomes directed to a particular sex who believes
in an initial free-floating or 'polymorphous' desire (The Essentials of
Psycho-Analysis 201), a sexuality that is disapproved of and regarded as
deviant. This disapproval often bases itself upon a common and culturally structured belief in the direct interrelationship between gender and
sexuality. Thus, biological givens are thought to be responsible for de-
termining people's sexual preferences. Any breaking of the rule would
be threatening to a secure zone of gender conformity. It can be assumed
sexuality operates in part through the stabilization of gender standards.
He proposes universalizing vision based on the idea that every human
being is bisexual and that sexual desire is characterized by mobility. He
thinks that all people are capable of making a homosexual object choice
whether in their sexual activities or in their unconscious. For Freud,
homosexual attraction is normal and he rejects all theories perceiving
homosexuals as sick and in need of psychotherapy, or those ideas that
regard homosexuals as a distinct sexual species like the third sex theory
discussed earlier. It has been found that all human beings are capable of
making a homosexual object choice and in fact have made one in their
unconscious. Indeed, libidinal attachments to persons of the same sex
play no less a part as factors in normal mental life, and a greater part as a
motive force for illness, than do similar attachments to the opposite sex.

This view separates gender from sexuality and disagrees with the
views articulated by the inversion model that supposes that homosexuality is the result of a mismatch between the individual's biological sex
and his psyche. This novel not only attests to the homosexual character's
struggle to find a place and be at peace with himself and with society.
Rather, it extends its insights to the suffering of various minority groups
throughout history. Prejudices often allow majorities to exert oppres-

sion over minorities since their position of power allows them to make judgements and classifications according to their standards of normality. The standard on which acceptance is based in this novel is that of American masculinity. As Baldwin explains:

> The American ideal, then, of sexuality appears to be rooted in the American ideal of masculinity. This ideal has created cowboys and Indians, good guys and bad guys, punks and studs, tough guys and softies, butch and faggots, black and white. It is an ideal so paralytically infantile that it is virtually forbidden- as an unpatriotic act- that the American boy evolves into the complexity of manhood. (James Baldwin and Sexuality 815)

In James Baldwin's novel *Another Country* the concept of whiteness, kill the African American male artist with words and actions. Sensitive, questioning, and talented, Baldwin's artist-heroes must free themselves of their socially constructed positions as African American men if they are to achieve their artistic goals. Because of his continual confrontational nature, the artist is aware that the possibility of death looms greater over him than any other figure in James Baldwin's fiction. In *Another Country* Rufus Scott succumbs to the power of whiteness and dies in the first third of the novel. The lesson is continued through the character of Eric Jones who learns to define and accept himself. Baldwin's triumphant protagonists resist being categorized in terms of their race and sexual orientation and ultimately embrace a more meaningful identity, that of the artist.

By making four of his principal characters artist-figures in *Another Country*, Baldwin argues for a consideration of how race, gender, and sexual orientation influence the artist-hero's journey toward self-definition and self acceptance. A central theme in *Another Country*, as in much of James Baldwin's work, is the struggle to acknowledge and accept all facets of oneself. The novel is explored through Rufus Scott, Baldwin's first artist-hero to embrace all aspects of his identity. The level of success that these characters attain is directly related to their desire and willingness to understand and accept themselves. In this chapter I will show how these two artists, one African American and one white, illustrate Baldwin's view that the artist-figure is doomed unless he goes by his natural propensity. *Another Country* (1962) examines the effect of race, sexuality, and discrimination on the artist and his mission.

The legacy of bitterness that the elder Baldwin passed on led the son to embark on a lifetime quest to understand and quell discrimination. Baldwin realizes that he must learn to channel these negative feelings if he is to survive. *Another Country* explores attempts to overcome that anger. In *Another Country* the question of identity haunts Rufus Scott who must decide how to handle his own bitterness which becomes too gruesome thing to live with.

Some of the characters in *Another Country* express the kind of frustration that Baldwin articulated in essays and interviews during the early 1960's In *The New Lost Generation* published in Esquire in 1961, Baldwin begins his reflection on the experience of exile with the story of a friend who commits suicide because the society around him was not ready to accept him in any way, the white dominated world stubbornly refuse his vision; it despised him for his vision and scourged him for his color. This friend, identified in interviews as Eugene, resembles Rufus Scott and Eric Jones, both central characters in *Another Country*. There are obvious similarities. Both Eugene and Rufus had white girlfriends and killed themselves by jumping off the George Washington Bridge. But there are also more subtle links. It appears that homosexual desires led both the real man and the fictional character to desperation. In *The Price of the Ticket* Baldwin recalls Eugene saying that he might be involved with him shortly before he committed suicide. In *Another Country* Eric Jones tells

Rufus Scott of his romantic feelings for him but here the confessor is redeemed by receiving the love he so desperately seeks.

Easily the most arresting character that Baldwin has created, Rufus Scott remains unforgettable largely because of the depth of his literal and figurative fall. *Another Country* begins on the last night of Rufus Scott's life. The first part of the novel serves as an explanation for Rufus' sense of despair. We witness his decline knowing, as he does, that there is no redemption in sight. Rufus has been roaming the streets of New York City for a month trying to cope with the physical and emotional pain he has inflicted on his lover Leona. He has not contacted his family or his friends and they are all worried about him. After nearly resorting to prostitution in order to eat, Rufus sees that his end has come, but simultaneously the feeling of being a man who holds equally his positions with his counterparts did also prevailed which later gave him a sense of identity and selfhood. Rufus drops in to visit his best friend, Vivaldo Moore, before taking his life. Rufus' descent comprises the first section of *Another Country*.

The fact that Rufus's artistic identity is formed by the time that we encounter him in the novel foreshadows his demise. The development of the hero as an artist is central to Baldwin's artist-narratives. John Grimes in *Go Tell It on the Mountain* and Sonny of Sonny's Blues have their futures assured primarily because we witness their struggle to define themselves. "Sonny's Blues" and *Go Tell It on the Mountain* both tell the story of young African American men who come to understand and accept themselves. This developmental element is missing in *Another Country*. We don't witness Rufus Scott's journey to the stage and are left wondering what led him to become a drummer. How did he make it to Greenwich Village from Harlem and what was his life like before he met Leona? Although it is clear from the only scene in the jazz club that Rufus had been a successful and respected drummer, he does not perform in *Another Country*. Rufus is in constant flight throughout the novel. He even joins the Navy in order to escape the streets of Harlem and the drugs and violence that threatened his future and prompted him to fled from a place which does not exist for him, the sense of insecurity which for that matter every black person actualised in their respective ways. What Rufus fears is as much a part of himself as his heart beat: his artistic fate, the paradoxical situation that Rufus is running from himself.

Unlike Baldwin's other artist figures, Rufus Scott is reduced to the role of voyeur in his artistic area. In the only scene in the novel in which Rufus plays with his band, a young horn player communicates his pain to the audience. Listeners become spellbound by the passion and fervour of his music.

> He stood there... Shivering in the rags of his twenty-odd years, and screaming through the horn do you love me? Do you love me? This, anyway, was the question Rufus heard, the same phrase, unbearably, endlessly and variously repeated, with all the force the boy had... And yet the question was terrible and real. (8-9)

In this question, Rufus repeatedly hears the pain and disillusionment that the young man experienced. The scene foreshadows Rufus's death as it marks the end of his career as a musician. Rufus stands as a witness to the rise of an artist who uses his life in his art. Rufus, not the anonymous saxophone player, should be utilizing his music to communicate the lessons that he has learned. Rufus must find the courage to play his blues. Later while listening to Bessie Smith singing, Rufus wonders how people manage to overcome the blues which echoed with a sense of relief and comfort to the troubled psyche long being ravished of its own aesthetics which is being accepted and endorsed with all its affiliations. The blues contain the possibility of salvation for Rufus. The fact that Rufus cannot transform his blues into art is the precise reason for his suicide.

The artist must articulate his blues through his art. At the end of his life Rufus cannot accomplish this feat and thus his failure is complete.

Because the geographical focus is on Greenwich Village and not on Harlem, perhaps *Another Country* is Baldwin's test of the integrationist policies of the 1950s. Both Rufus and Ida Scott attempt to realize their artistic goals in the white world of Greenwich Village and midtown Manhattan. Yet both characters become pawns in someone else's sexual fantasy. They cannot escape the sexual stereotypes of African Americans and are seen respectively as the black buck and the Jezebel. Ida Scott personifies the rage of African Americans during the 1960s. Blaming white America for her brother's death, Ida turns her relationships with the white characters in the novel to her advantage. Thus Ida Scott's tenuous standing as a jazz vocalist emerges from the opinion of her peers, jazz musicians. She hasn't endured the tumult she undergoes during the process.

Anger consumes Rufus, leaving no room for art, family, love or even his own humanity. His cry, 'You took the best so why not take the rest?' is the sign of his inability to fight racism, to fight stereotypes, to uphold his humanity. The best to which Rufus refers is all that he has lost: his life as a musician, his role as a respected member of his Harlem community and the community of musicians, and his own self-respect.

Rufus Scott's sense of his powerlessness is shown in his relationships with his friends and his lover. He surrounds himself with white people. Rufus' easy acquisition of Leona, his white girlfriend, leads him to madness. He becomes convinced that Leona dates him because of the stereotype of African American men as well endowed: "She loves colored folks so much…sometimes I just can't stand it. You know all that chick knows about me? The only thing she knows?' He put his hand on his sex, brutally as though he would tear it out" (68). He doesn't want to accept the possibility that Leona might actually love him for himself. Never able to forget his race, Rufus offers quite alarming dealings with white women during his Greenwich Village years where while interacting with the white girls who made him realise that black color of him is unacceptable in all possible ways. Rufus' unconscious acceptance of the role of black stud and of the superiority of white women leads to his decreasing self-esteem.

Rufus' irrationality is not the derangement of the criminally insane, but the madness of one who is constantly assaulted because of his race. After a particularly violent fight with Leona, his white girlfriend Rufus is confronted by his best friend Vivaldo Moore who threatens him to keep a distance from white people otherwise consequences would be dangerous, the remarks that were quite disgusting. Rufus sees the power of whiteness as the force which inhibits his ability to live his life as he chooses. Whiteness, which translates to power and oppression, fuels his rage.

Rufus Scott's hatred of whites, particularly Southerners, may be traced to his Harlem upbringing and his military stint in the South. Yet the source of Rufus' sexual and physical abuse of these characters is their whiteness, their skin color and all that it represents to Rufus. Only as he descends into his self-made hell does Rufus realize the connections between his relationships with Eric and Leona. "He remembered," Baldwin writes, only that… Eric had loved him; as he now remembered that Leona had loved him. He had despised Eric's manhood treating him as a woman, by telling him how inferior he was to a woman, by treating him as nothing more than a hideous sexual deformity. But Leona had not been a deformity. And he had used against her the very epithets he had used against Eric, and in the very same way, with the same roaring in his head and the same intolerable pressure in his chest (47). Rufus responds to Eric and Leona's whiteness and not their affection for him. Although they are his lovers, Eric and Leona come to symbolize the power of whiteness, the power that has been denied to Rufus.

At the beginning of *Another Country* Rufus Scott is in the midst of his descent. Alone and alienated from his family and friends, Rufus must learn to use his isolation to come to terms with his fears. Rufus had been a successful jazz drummer before he met Leona. They immediately embark upon a sexual relationship that ultimately destroys them both. Rufus' sense of powerlessness is diametrically opposed to Sonny's experience in *Sonny's Blues.*

You walk these streets, black and funky and cold, and there's not really a living ass to talk to and there's nothing shaking, and there's no way of getting it out – that storm inside. You can't talk it and you can't make love with it, and when you finally try to get with it and play it, you realize nobody's listening. So you've got to listen. You got to find a way to listen (115). Like Sonny, Rufus Scott finds himself walking the streets and dealing with "confronting that storm inside." But, unlike Sonny, Rufus doesn't try to understand and conquer the pain. This inner conflict leads Rufus to avoid his family in Harlem and causes him to physically and emotionally abuse his white girlfriend. He simply walks blindly through the streets of Manhattan hoping that the pain will cease. Perhaps now, though, he had hit bottom… yet there knocked in his heart the suspicion that the bottom did not really exist … He wanted to stand up, breathe, and at the same time he wanted to lie flat on the floor and be swallowed into whatever would stop this pain. Yet he was aware that nothing would stop it, nothing: this was himself….Nor did he understand what force within this body had driven him into such a desolate place (153-154).

Through Baldwin's initial focus on Rufus Scott, as examined the ways in which following social norms lead to a denial of identity and ultimately to death for the African American male bisexual. "Baldwin is careful to make all his characters bisexual faggots", by which Baldwin means exclusively and effeminately homosexual" (p165). After reading

Baldwin's Giovanni's Room, Joseph Beam, a gay black man and writer, wondered if there was any hope for the future. 'Could there be any happy endings in this kind of love?' In *Another Country* James Baldwin asks readers to consider what motivate Rufus Scott, a bisexual man, to throw himself off the George Washington Bridge and why Eric Jones, a white homosexual, flourishes. Sadly Rufus clings to socially constructed definitions of himself rather than defining and accepting himself. Because he cannot acknowledge his bisexuality and his love for two white people, Rufus turns his love into hatred. Instead of focusing on his own feelings, Rufus destroys those who love him. Rufus despised him because he came from Alabama perhaps he had allowed Eric to make love to him in order to despise him more completely. Rufus' violence towards Eric, and perhaps Leona, stems from being attacked by a Southern Army officer during his youth. James Baldwin expressed his thoughts on homosexuality and race in a 1986 interview with Richard Goldstein of the Village Voice. It can be surmised that black person who is simultaneously gay is just like the conundrum to the society, threatened, menaced and time to time reminded that he is black, his color is disgusting and has no right to live in a society lived by white people.

Indeed. It is the "question of color" which leads Rufus Scott to commit suicide though his denial of his sexual feelings and acknowledgment of the sexual acts he performs with Eric play an important role, because throughout his life that he is black and for that matter every black person to be accepted has to pay a huge price, a price to be humiliated now and then and in a sense lead a wretched life of self hatred never at peace him himself/herself. Rufus has sex with Eric and Leona because he wants their love, but he sees himself as being unworthy of anyone's love. Walking the streets of New York City and contemplating prostituting himself makes Rufus think of Eric: "He glimpsed, for the first time, the extent, the nature, of Eric's loneliness and the danger in which this placed him;

and wished that he had been nicer to him" (45). Rufus' own loneliness, compounded by the fact that he has distanced himself from Eric and all those who care about him, leads him to kill himself.

Recent research shows that suicide is surprisingly common among African Americans, citing the decrease of cultural ties due to the migration of African Americans from rural to urban environments, however it is generally estimated that during white color renaissance that the African American male is increasingly displaced who were at much greater risk for suicide than black females, not only are black males more likely than females to be involved in deviant and self destructive behaviour they are also less likely to complete high school and to be employed.

When we first encounter Rufus, he is unemployed and homes. The story of how he descended to this level is told in flashbacks during the first third of the novel. Through his relationship with Leona and his final tragic state, we see how Rufus Scott fits Major's description. Rufus feels as though he failed his family and is ashamed to face them. As he rides the train, Rufus considers getting off in Harlem to visit his family but continues north. He departs the train at the George Washington Bridge. It is here that Rufus commits suicide.

Though suicide is often presented as a viable option for African American men in James Baldwin's fiction, Rufus Scott's taking of his own life is the only such depiction in Baldwin's fiction. Rufus is characterized by a sense of hopelessness and despair that is unmatched by the other artist heroes. He is unable to address his fear. Peter in "Previous Condition" and Sonny in "Sonny's Blues" acknowledge and accept the possibility that their quests might end in death or madness.

Describing life for the African American man in such stark life or death terms is overly dramatic, but then their plight seems to call for such a response. Rufus's homelessness is more than physical; he is emotionally and spiritually lost. The deprivation of faith, often associated with a belief in love in Baldwin's fiction, is a major contributing factor to Rufus' suicide.

By committing suicide, Rufus Scott maintains some measure of control over his destiny and continues to do battle with white racism. The act of throwing himself off the George Washington Bridge is foreshadowed throughout the first section of the novel. Rufus seems to hear the Hudson River calling to him as he remembers a childhood drowning victim. His final words, "all right, you mother fucking Godal mighty bastard, I'm coming to you,"(p 88) signal his surrender to what he perceives as white, racist forces (Rufus' suicide evokes the images of slaves who drowned themselves during the Middle Passage rather than endure further horrors of slavery. His suicide is also an act of defiance and illustrates his empowerment. Just as Morrison's Seth kills her daughter in part to retain some control over the quality of life for her child, Rufus finally takes control over the way in which he wants to live or die. With his thoughts on the bridge, Rufus comes closest to articulating his blues and certainly Rufus's experience, resonates throughout the remainder of the novel as the other characters try to comprehend his actions.

Reading Baldwin's artist heroes as responses to Wright's Bigger Thomas allows for a contextualization of some of the more distressing aspects of Rufus Scott. In *Another Country* Rufus Scott is reminiscent of Richard Wright's archetypal figure, Bigger Thomas. The physical abuse Rufus inflicts upon hi white Southern lover marks Rufus' descent into Wright's Bad Nigger archetype. Although Baldwin's sensitive portrayal of an African American man consumed with stereotypical notions about his gender and race is sympathetic.

Unfortunately, many of Baldwin's characters do not live in communities wherein they are reminded of their humanity; as a result, Baldwin says, they end up lying in "wine and urine-stained hallways" not knowing that they "are very beautiful"(James Baldwin "Down at the Cross,"1963,

1). Baldwin predicts that humanity, if it does not work to stop this loss of beauty, will see the arrival one day of "cosmic vengeance," It is a vengeance that cannot really be executed by, any person or organization, and for that matter cannot be prevented by any police force or army, it is a historical vengeance, based on the law that that can be recognized provided human beings learn to respect and value other people despite their color, and creed.

In America, this day of cosmic vengeance may be staved off if individuals of various racial backgrounds choose to fashion ideologies and to institute practices that acknowledge the human worth of all citizens. If this is not done and false notions of human inferiority and superiority persist, Baldwin says cosmic vengeance may be inevitable: If we—and now I mean the relatively conscious whites and the relatively conscious blacks, who must, like lovers, insist on, or create, the consciousness of the others—do not falter in our duty now, we may be able, handful that we are, to end the racial nightmare, and achieve [the goals of] our country, and change the history of the world. If we do not now dare everything, the fulfillment of that prophecy, created from the Bible in song by a slave, is upon us: 'God gave Noah the rainbow sign, No more water, the first next time!'("Down at the Cross" 4)

Speaking of flood and fire, Baldwin uses biblical terms to characterize the coming day of cosmic vengeance, alluding to the destruction of the world by floodwaters as recorded in Genesis and referring to the prophetic end of the world by fire as recorded in Revelation. For Baldwin, these are not literal but metaphorical, a way to characterize the fall of a social order, based in greed and human inequality. Coming from a fire-and-brimstone evangelical tradition, however, he is doubtless aware that in Revelation 21:8, the biblical writer John prophecies that God in the end times will establish a new heaven and earth, burning in the lake of fire those who have lived in defiance of God's will. Black people were taken to be traitors, with a gruelling, agonizing, the most shameful, fanatical, fawning, sycophantic love of the whites the tendency which could destroy so much, never failed to destroy the man who hated and this was an immutable law. But in the racial stratification of American private and public life, hatred was only one ingredient—is only one ingredient (Baldwin's work withstands translation to the present tense)—and not a necessary one. The country's race nightmare could not be examined in isolation, like quadrennial election issues such as immigration policy or Social Security. Race was—is—the fundamental American issue, underlying not only all matters of public policy (economic inequality, criminal justice, housing, education) but the very psyche of the nation. "The country's image of the Negro," Baldwin writes in *Nobody Knows My Name*, "which hasn't very much to do with the Negro, has never failed to reflect with a kind of frightening accuracy the state of mind of the country" (12).

The Biblical fearful, and unbelieving, abominable and whoremongers will be taken to task and a situation will prevail when society's oppressed and marginalized will pour forth angrily, ready to slum down the chaos and actualize the dawn of curtain on the American dream, this dream being the unfulfilled promise that all American citizens are equal and have a right to life, liberty, and the pursuit of happiness long been denied to black intelligentsia.

This fiery revolt will come when the marginalized, having spent many years waiting for a fairer, more equitable day, realize that those in power are unwilling to change. Already, according to Baldwin, the rumblings of such a revolt are coming from marginalized individuals who are creating new ideologies to replace those that have oppressed and dehumanized them

Baldwin's use of two dominant artist-heroes in *Another Country* lends itself to an examination of the impact of race and sexuality on the maturation process of the artist-figure. Despite the variable of race, both Rufus Scott and Eric Jones must undergo a revelatory experience in order to be reborn as artists. Refuting stereotypes based on race or sexual orientation and adopting instead a primary identification as an artist is the first sign of the requisite reawakening of the artist-hero. The transformation or the lack thereof determines the nature of ensuing artistic experience. This awakening is particularly important for Rufus Scott because, as an African American male, his humanity is constantly called into question. Houston Baker, echoing Baldwin's concern for African American male characters to accept their humanity, identifies the primary cause of Rufus' death ,apparently paid a price of being black, a legacy which blacks are long been sharing bequeathed to them by the white masters mostly symbolised b y the Leon in the novel. Rufus not only battles with the ideology passed on by Leona' forefathers but he ultimately loses his life in the process. Rufus Scott's descent is paralleled by Eric Jones's ascent in *Another Country*.

Eric Jones emerges as Baldwin's most successful artist-hero. Because of his personal struggles, he becomes a model of honesty for the other characters in *Another Country*. The only son of a wealthy Alabama couple, Eric is burdened with the weight of his parents' high expectations almost from birth. Right from early days knows that he is different and that different means wrong.

The trouble with a secret life is that it is very frequently a secret from the person who lives it and not at all a secret for the people he encounters. He encounters, because he *must* encounter, those people who see his secrecy before they see anything else, and who drag these secrets out of him; sometimes with the intention of using them against him, sometimes with more benevolent intent; but, whatever the intent, the moment is awful and the accumulating revelation is an unspeakable anguish. The aim of the dreamer, after all, is merely to go on dreaming and not to be molested by the world. His dreams are his protection against the world. But the aims of life are antithetical to those of the dreamer, and the teeth of the world are sharp. How could Eric have known that his fantasies, however unreadable they were for him, were inscribed in every one of his gestures, were betrayed in every inflection of his voice, and lived in his eyes with all the brilliance and beauty and terror of desire? He had always been a heavy, healthy boy, had played like other children, and fought as they did, made friends and enemies and secret pacts and grandiose plans. And yet none of his playmates, after all, had ever sat with Henry in the furnace room, or ever kissed Henry on his salty face. They did not, weighed down with discarded hats, gowns, bags, sashes, earrings, capes, and necklaces, turn themselves into make-believe characters after everyone in their house was asleep. Nor could they possibly, at their most extended, have conceived of the people he, in the privacy of night, became: his mother's friends, or his mother — his mother as he conceived her to have been when she was young, his mother's friends as his mother was now; the heroines and heroes of the novels he read, and the movies he saw; or people he simply put together out of his fantasies and the available rags. No doubt, at school, the boy with whom he was wrestling failed to feel the curious stabs of terror and pleasure that Eric felt, as they grappled with each other, as one boy pinned the other to the ground; and if Eric saw the girls at all, he saw mainly their clothes and their hair; they were not, for him, as were the boys, creatures in a hierarchy, to be adored or feared or despised. None of them looked on each other as he looked on all of them. His dreams were different subtly and cruelly and criminally-different: this was not known yet, but it was felt. He was menaced in a way that they were not, and it was perhaps this sense, and the instinct which compels people to move away from the doomed, which accounted for the invincible distance, increasing with the years, which stretched between himself and his contemporaries.

Yet Eric's freedom lies in his rejection of a secret life. His first homosexual relationship frees him from the prison of his Southern hometown and his indifferent parents and it will surely take many years to pass to accept what the hideous obsequiousness of people who despised him but who did not dare to say so, started to dawn on him to discover himself. Eric's painful journey toward self-acceptance is the single most important factor in his later success. Eric's expression of his sexual self fuels his artistic liberation.

The road to self-love is a long and arduous one for Eric. Finding the strength to acknowledge and accept his identity as a homosexual and as an actor is the quality that makes Eric Jones the principal subject of *Another Country*. He does so in France and this act of courage is the source of Eric's power. The fact that neither Eric nor Rufus can achieve a sense of wholeness in New York City is Baldwin's commentary on the restricting nature of life in the United States. In "The New Lost Generation" (James Baldwin196).Baldwin contemplates the impact exile had on his life which was undeniably feasible for Baldwin to groom and grow artistically and made to the world to actualise his point of view very aesthetically and maturely for that matter. The distance the artist-hero travels should be in search of self, not in flight from self. It is significant that, for Eric to find out who he was, he had to leave New York City and the United States.

Notwithstanding Like James Baldwin, Eric Jones gains a new, deeper sense of himself in France. Although Eric's embrace of his sexual identity in Europe alters his life, he realizes that he must return to the United States if he is to measure his success: "Why am I going home? He asked himself. But he knew why. It was time. In order not to lose all that he had gained, he had to move forward and risk it all" (230). His renewed sense of self helps his acting career. Eric Jones' sexuality and profession, possible weapons for his enemies, are transformed instead into tools of empowerment.

In Paris Eric learns the meaning of love which he realised that very human being is capable of love but unfortunately, many have crippled themselves with all kinds of belief systems, opinions, philosophies, ideologies – everything except life. Human beings are capable of love when they are willing. Unfortunately, we want to export everything that is beautiful in our life to heaven and live wantonly on this planet. Love, joy, blissfulness – these are human possibilities. Eric prospers because he is able not only to love himself but to accept himself. By defining himself, Eric achieves the only kind of success that is valued: the love and acceptance of self. Therefore, best efforts were made on his behalf to create standards and built an aura of self confidence to go along and consciously ensure himself about the people to be sought after and to be avoided. This definition of love is closely related to what I see as James Baldwin's vision of art. Honesty is the most important element in both artistic and love relationships.

An important indication of Eric's success as a human being and as an artist is his ability to share his hard-won self love and acceptance with others. Baldwin casts him as a healer, one who heals through love, *in Another Country.* All who are intimate with him find themselves transformed. Eric has brief love affairs with Cass Silenski, a middle class wife and mother, and Vivaldo Moore, a young writer. Vivaldo, who has had sexual encounters with men in the past, understands that he is basically heterosexual, but his experience with Eric changes him. "So what can we really do for each other except – just love each other and be each other's witness?....So that we can really stretch into whoever we are?" (p 396). Love, like art, not only liberates but nurtures. Fueled by honesty, it leads to positive developments. After a sexual "conversion" by Eric during which he discovers new meaning in his life, Vivaldo resumes his writing and his characters speak to him. His life as a successful artist begins. His writing, which had not been going well, begins to flourish. Vivaldo gains insight into his writing and his romantic relationship with Ida Scott. He finally acknowledges the futility of his relationship with Ida Scott. With its focus on Eric Jones and Rufus Scott, *Another country* is a critique of conventional notions of masculinity. All of the male characters, with the exception of Eric Jones, struggle with the way in which masculinity is constructed in the United States and each of them ultimately rejects narrow definitions of a gendered self. Even the minor characters Vivaldo Moore and Richard Silenski change their views of themselves as men. Richard had been Vivaldo's high school English teacher and the two are engaged in a subtle competition. Each man has been writing a novel for years, but Richard secretly finishes his novel and presents Vivaldo with a published copy. Richard Silenski's community of family and friends lose respect for him as a writer because they recognize the lack of truth and artistic effort in his commercially successful novel. Richard defines himself by his roles as a father, husband, and provider. He is forced to re-examine his life when his wife commits adultery with a bisexual man. Vivaldo Moore, a minor character, may not be a commercially successful writer like Richard Silenski but we, as readers, respect him as an artist because we see the internal struggle and self-examination which he undergoes in order to write fiction. He learns to listen to those voices he had previously tried to silence and this development leads him to begin writing his novel in earnest. Through his sexual experience with Eric, Vivaldo redefines himself in terms of his vocation and his masculinity.

Rufus Scott's restricted definition of masculinity excludes his unacknowledged homosexual acts with Eric. It is significant that, at the end of his life, Rufus thinks of Eric and regrets the ways in which he punished Eric for helping him to reveal his own homosexual desires. Rufus must disavow his feelings for Eric in order to remain "black" and "male" in his own eyes and in the eyes of the African American community. This adherence to rigid cultural standards leads Rufus to deny his affection for Eric and thus submerge a part of himself. Rufus exemplifies that negation of homosexuality implies state's efforts to universalize heterosexual culture and to construct a masculine identity. He challenges this heterosexual and masculine identity of America to preserve both white and black culture in its own way which if left untouched would surely boomerang the whole society.

Therefore, while confronting the fear of being different becomes the acceptance of a personal identity and carrying the hash tag of queer unlike the indecisive David in *Giovanni's Room*, the men in *Another Country* are forced to make decisions about their sexuality if they are to survive. In his study of gay self-representation in literature, David Bergman asserts that a negative identity becomes 'an absence of identity.' In other words there is no identity without a homosexual one. Eric Jones contradicts Bergman's argument when he delivers the message of the novel that to achieve the highest regards of life along with its sublime niceties; one has to be genuine and true to it, lest it is not possible to grapple with it or vision about it. The responsibility of whether to live a life of truth or a life of lies clearly is the domain of the artist. Eric is determined to live life fully and honestly and it is this sense of completeness that the other characters in the novel seek.

In *Just Above My Head* (1979), Joel is unique among Baldwin's characters for he represents, at different times, both groups. During the preaching days of his daughter Julia he lives as one insanely mad, so engrossed with his daughter's divine calling that he stands unconcerned, not only about the neglect and oppression of his son Jimmy, but also about the oppression surrounding his own life as a black man in a racist society. After Julia's preaching days, Joel becomes a member of the bitterly mad, seeing everything and everyone, especially his daughter, as conspiring to keep him down and running away from his responsibilities.

Unlike Joel, those who respond properly to oppression become heroes. They refuse to grow bitter as a result of thinking only about their oppressors. Yet, they also refuse to divorce faith from daily living and do not ignore the social ramifications of oppression in their lives and the lives of other marginalized peoples. Rather, they walk middle ground, acknowledging oppression while striving for a life that regards others as their equal.

Figuratively, they, like Fonny in *If Beale Street Could Talk* (1974), build a table of Fellowship even as they sit in jail because of the false accusations of a racist police officer. Keeping faith in their own humanity and resisting defeat or despair because of terrible social wrong, they are able to hold on to their human selves. This balanced response is the prescription Baldwin gives to those who would survive oppression, regardless of when or whether society erupts into the chaos and fire of bitter revolution.

Eric's open acknowledgement and acceptance of his multiple identities silences those who would persecute him. By embracing both his masculine and feminine qualities, Eric Jones personifies Baldwin's philosophy of love. Eric Jones has found fulfillment in his personal and professional lives while remaining clear about his sexuality, Vivaldi sees these qualities when he watches Eric at work. ". . . This masculinity was defined, and made powerful by something which was not masculine. But it was not feminine either. . . . it was a face which suggested, resonantly, in the depth, the truth about our natures" (330). Eric personifies masculinity, femininity, strength, and vulnerability. His ability not only to embody all these qualities but to express them is another factor in his success as an artist-hero.

The many depictions of sexual relationships in the novel have garnered more attention than Baldwin's exploration of the artist figure. The fascination that surrounds black sexuality overshadows any aesthetic concerns. In *Another Country* sex operates much in the same fashion that love does in James Baldwin's works. It becomes a symbol of self-acceptance and personal growth and is something that takes on a transcendent quality.

What is uncovered by focusing on the meaning and legacy of Rufus Scott in *Another Country* is that without this quest for self, without "going the way your blood beats,... you won't live any life at all"(185). Eric Jones possesses the courage to examine himself and so he joins Sonny in representing the quality of honesty in life and art that characterizes the successful Baldwin artist-hero. We believe that the novel becomes a sanctuary for James Baldwin as he ages. It is a place for his to explore his position as an artist, as an African American, as a man. Certainly, the *Another Country, Tell Me How Long the Train's Been Gone,* and *Just Above My Head* are all studies of the creative person in various stages of development and of the factors which affect his self-image. More and more frequently the novel becomes the place for Baldwin to interrogate and analyze his own fragile position as a writer and his more accepted, though unwanted, stature as a racial spokesperson. In his next novel *Tell Me How Long the Train's Been Gone,* James Baldwin examines the meaning of the artist who flees from truth and ends up in a prison of his own making.

3

Conclusion

In his effort to illuminate the darkness, Baldwin claims, that all human beings, regardless of factors such as race, nationality, and social status, are innately and equally human. He even suggests, like many in the African-American faith tradition and like biblical writers such as the Apostle Paul, that human equality is natural, is divinely mandated. And as such, human equality, or at least the proclamation of it, particularly in written discourse, is the proclamation of truth itself. Yet, for all those proclaiming truth, that is, human equality, there are still those who stand as advocates of falsehood, insisting upon the lesser humanity of certain individuals, vociferously Baldwin shows in *Go Tell It on the Mountain* (1953), *Giovanni's Room* (1956), *If Beale Street Could Talk* (1974), and *Just Above My Head* (1978) how those advocates of falsehood, empowered as members of various modern social institutions, use false narratives to further their belief that all people are not divinely created, that all do not possess the potential to develop into their ideal human selves. Baldwin suggests that their narratives, which are found in a variety of places, from newspaper articles to police reports, attempt to dismiss human equality as a philosophical truth by divorcing narrative subjects from any sort of historical context. Fighting against such oversimplifications and prejudices, Baldwin uses his novels to provide proper historical context and thereby reveal the humanity of the characters who serve as subjects of his narratives.

The tragic element of Baldwin's art is that often knowledge of the humanity of these characters is known only by readers of his novels, not by the society he portrays. Only readers of Baldwin's novels possess this privileged information. Within the fictional societies of Baldwin's novels, the dehumanizing false images of certain characters are considered by society at large as accurate representations of who the characters are. These false images cause characters great suffering. In other words, because the characters are portrayed as being less than human, they are treated unjustly, inhumanly and often succumb to the negative images imposed on them. Baldwin reveals, however, how sometimes unjust treatment actually pushes people into becoming more, not less, than their human selves. In their suffering, these characters gain insight into their humanity and as a result, feel compelled to serve other sufferers so that they too might remember that they are fully endowed human beings.

As such, Baldwin reveals the important role of service in the lives of those who must fight, perhaps more than some, to believe that they are human. In valuing service, Baldwin aligns himself with the Christian-based faith tradition he embraced as a youth. As an adult, though deeply frustrated with what he perceived to be the unloving character both of the black Pentecostal church wherein he had served as a boy preacher and of the Christian church in general, Baldwin still valued service, service being the essence of spirituality within Judeo-Christianity. In writing about this, Baldwin also reveals to many in the black literary establishment who define spirituality solely within the realm of the supernatural or the church that spirituality also manifests itself in the way in which communities are shown to be places of conversation and caring and in the way individuals serve one another, reminding each other that they are human beings, not beasts nor devils. The deeper principles of Christian thought, he shows, are accepting of all, giving to all, and spirituality is not confined to the realm of either the supernatural or the established church.

Baldwin succeeded in establishing the Negro experience as of immediate relevance to a society concerned with the problem of identity or alienation. His art would supply the black pride which would free the blacks from the psychological enslavement they have endured for more than two centuries in an essentially racist white society. He showed that black community was in urgent need of justice and brotherhood. Therefore, James Baldwin achieved authentic dramatizations of the black identity and experience and his goal was the elimination of racism in America.

The artist functions as a social palliative and corrective. He alone is capable of striking a balance between the images of Americans both black and white with the truth about them, which they try to evade. He is committed to disturb the complacency of the people and to prepare them to deal with the calamity. His objectivity enables him to perceive the realities and to illuminate the defects of the society. In its sensitivity to shades of discrimination and moral shape, and in its commitment despite everything to America, his voice was comparable in importance to that of any person of letters from recent decades.

Works Consulted

- Baldwin, James. *Giovanni's Room.* New York: Dial Press, 1956 Print.
- - - - Nobody Knows My Name. New York: Dial Press, 1961.
- - - -. *Go Tell It On The Mountain.* New York: Dial Press, 1962 Print.
- - - -. *Another Country.* New York: Dial Press, 1962 Print.
- - - - Blues for Mister Charlie. New York: Dial Press, 1964.
- - - - The Amen Comer. New York: Dial Press, 1968.
- - - -. *Tell Me How Long The Train's Been Gone.* New York: Dial Press, 1968 Print
- - - -. *If Beale Street Could Talk.* New York: Dial Press, 1974 Print.
- - - -. *Just Above My Head.* New York: Dial Press, 1979 Print.
- -- -The Price of the Ticket. New York: St Matin's/ Marek,1985.
- - - - "Down at the Cross". Notes of a Native Son. Boston: Beacon Press, 1955.
- Butterfield, Stephen. Black Autobiography in America. Amherst: The University of Massachusetts Press, 1974. Print
- Christian, Barbara. "Diminishing Returns: Can Black Feminism(s) Survive the Academy?" *In Multiculturalism: A Critical Reader*, ed. David Theo Goldberg, 168–79. Cambridge: Basil Blackwell
- DuBois , W. E. B. *Souls of the Black Folk.* Chicago: AC.McClurg and Co., 1903. Print.

- - - -. The Crisis. Vol.22.June (1921).55.Print.
- Eckman, Fern Marja. *The Furious Passage of James Baldwin.* New York :M. Evans & Co., 1966.Print. Print.
- Freud, Sigmund. "The Uncanny," *An Infantile Neurosis and Other Works*, vol. XVII, *The Complete Psychological Works of Sigmund Freud.* trans. James Strachey (London: The Hogarth Press, 1977). Print.
- Gates, Henry Louis (1987a): *Figures in Black. Words, Signs, and the "Racial" Self.* New York: Oxford University Press. (1987)
- Hughes, Langston. "The Nation", Vol. 122 No.3181 (1926). Print.
- Johnson, Charles Richard. *Being and Race: Black Writing Since 1970.* CA: Indiana University Press, 1988. Print.
- Karenga, Maulana."Du bois and the color line: Race and class in the age of globalization". Social and Democracy. Vol.17(1): 141-160. Jan 2003.Print.
- Locke, Alain. "The New Negro."***The New Negro.*** Ed. Alain Locke. New York: Antheneum, 1968. 5-16. Print
- Lorde, Audre. *Sister outsider: Essays and Speeches.* New York: Crossing Press, 1984.Print.
- Mc Dowell, Deborah E. *The Changing Same: Black Women's Literature, Criticism, and Theory.* Bloomington: Indiana U P. 1995. Print.
- Peirce, James Mills Professor X. 1897. [Letter]. In Sexual Inversion, by Havelock Ellis and John Addington Symonds, 273–275. London: Wilson and Macmillan. Facsimile reprint, New York: Arno Press, 1975.)
- Shin, Andrew, and Barbara Hudson. "Beneath the Black aesthetic: James Baldwin's Primer of Black American Masculinity

- Afican American Gay Author." African American Review. Summer 1998

- Smith, Barbara. "Toward a black feminist criticism." In Hull: 157-175, 1982. Print

- Watson, Steven. *The Harlem Renaissance*. New York: Pantheon, 1995. Print.

Periodicals

"Sonny's Blues." Partisan Review, Summer 1957.

"The New Lost Generation." Esquire, July 1961.

"We Be Fresh As Hell Wit' Da Feds Watchin': A Bad Black Debate Family Responds" Department of Communication University of Pittsburgh 06 Sunday October 2013.

Muzafar Ahmad Bhat is a Ph.D Scholar in the department of English at Annamalai University, Tamil Nadu- one of the oldest and most reputed institutions in India. He has published several articles in national and international journals.

www.ingramcontent.com/pod-product-compliance
Lightning Source LLC
LaVergne TN
LVHW050541200726
843506LV00001B/58